PENGUIN BOOKS

COMPUTER BITS AND

Geoff Simons has written a wide range of books – dealing with such topics as superstition, witchcraft, sexology and censorship – but is perhaps best known for his books on computers. His twelve books in this field cover microprocessors, industrial robots, privacy, the development of fifth-generation computers, and the treatment of women in the computer industry. In addition, he has published well over a hundred articles in the technical and general press. At present he is exploring whether computers can be regarded as an emerging life-form. He has published a book on this, with others to follow.

He is married with four children and is currently employed as Chief Editor in a national computing organization. His particular interests include philosophy, artificial intelligence, current affairs, discussion and squash. He also enjoys food, films and 'free-thinking in the broadest sense'. *Computer Bits and Pieces* is his twenty-second published book.

Geoff Simons

Computer Bits and Pieces
A COMPENDIUM OF CURIOSITIES

'Well, here's to computer dating. Let's hope they iron out the bugs soon. . .'

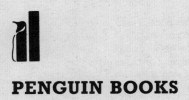

PENGUIN BOOKS

Penguin Books Ltd, Harmondsworth, Middlesex, England
Viking Penguin Inc., 40 West 23rd Street, New York, New York 10010, U.S.A.
Penguin Books Australia Ltd, Ringwood, Victoria, Australia
Penguin Books Canada Ltd, 2801 John Street, Markham, Ontario, Canada L3R 1B4
Penguin Books (N.Z.) Ltd, 182–190 Wairau Road, Auckland 10, New Zealand

First published 1984

For permission to reproduce cartoons thanks are due to:
Noel Ford, Martin Honeysett, Richard Howell and Geoff Rowley

Made and printed in Great Britain by
Hazell Watson & Viney Ltd, Aylesbury, Bucks
Set in Linotron 202 Bembo with Rockwell display by
Wyvern Typesetting Ltd, Bristol

Contents

Introduction

Have you heard of computers? They have probably heard of you. You are probably nicely filed away somewhere in the electronic bowels of some machine or other, working for the Inland Revenue, the social security department . . . or the police. And keeping track of you is not their only talent: computers are also finding out what they can do in factories, the home and outer space. They are nothing if not versatile. Like the human brain, they can be turned to this, that and the other – and there are minuscule computer systems (the size of a thumbnail) and mighty computer configurations (covering several acres). They also labour under a certain moral confusion: while working to diagnose disease and teach our children, they prepare to destroy the world.

We know that bank statements and electricity bills are prepared by computers, and that they can lurk in video systems and washing-machines. But do we always realize that computers can be imaginative poets, wizards at chemical analysis, writers of thrillers, creative mathematicians and world-champion games players? And what do we know about robots, the emerging families of artificial bodies, sprouting limbs and computer brains? We are now seeing robots that climb stairs, work in libraries, walk on the sea-bed; sighted robots that dust the furniture and solve Rubik's Cube; robots with fingers, eyes and sensitive skin; robots to converse with; robots playing cards and pouring drinks. And it may be that robots and computers are beginning to develop under their own steam, with a strange inertia that their human parents only partially understand. We are starting to be surprised at *how much* intelligent machines can actually do!

This book – aiming to inform, amuse and entertain – shows something of the immense variety of computer and robot uses in the world today. Thus it profiles the wide-ranging competence of today's intelligent machines. In no way is the book intended to be an exhaustive compilation. It is a collection of cameos, an insight into one of the most fascinating areas of modern technology.

1. The Historical Machine

'He creates them in his own image'

The Life-size Automaton

Albertus Magnus (1204–72) is said to have constructed a life-size automaton servant, and there are various accounts of what happened to it. One report declares that when Thomas Aquinas met the fellow in the street he smashed it to pieces, thinking it to be the work of the devil. Albertus is said to have complained that he thus destroyed the work of twenty years. In another account, the automaton was supposed to have been made out of metal, wood, glass, wax and leather. It was able to open the door to visitors and talk to them.

The Robot Francine

René Descartes (1596–1650) was inclined to believe that whereas animals were machines which may one day be duplicated or simulated by some mechanical means, human beings were different. It is a popular doctrine. Descartes had difficulty in imagining artefacts that could talk or reason: perhaps he would have been unhappy in the second half of the twentieth century. It is a fact that some of the central aims of modern research into artificial intelligence focus on what Descartes reckoned were the 'special characteristics of the human soul'. Despite all this, Descartes himself seemingly possessed an automaton, a young woman called Francine who accompanied Descartes on his travels. It is said that perhaps the robot was intended to resemble an illegitimate daughter of Descartes, from whom he was unhappily separated (her name too was Francine). Alas, a superstitious ship's captain, discovering the robot Francine in a packing-case, became alarmed and threw the automaton overboard. Little is known about this robot or about Descartes' attitude to it.

The Pascaline and Other Calculators

Blaise Pascal (1623–62) built one of the first mechanical calculating machines. He declared: 'I submit to the public a small machine of my own invention by means of which alone you may, without effort, perform all the operations of arithmetic, and may be relieved of the work which has often-times fatigued your spirit.' The Pascaline, built in 1642, was to be the first of many mechanical devices that would prove useful in evolving the logical theory upon which modern electronic computers would later be based. Wilhelm Gottfried von Leibniz (1646–1716) built a calculating machine that could multiply, add, divide and work out square roots. And a Minsk clockmaker, Jewna Jacobson, built a machine in 1770 that could compute numbers up to five digits. But perhaps *most* of the publicity has gone to Charles Babbage for his nineteenth-century calculating 'engines'.

The Babbage 'Engines'

Charles Babbage (1792–1871) built his Difference Engine in 1823 and spent the last forty years of his life trying, without success, to perfect his Analytical Engine. The Difference Engine was the first mechanical device to produce tables for navigation, insurance and astronomy. Of the Analytical Engine, Ada Lovelace, Babbage's co-worker, remarked that it 'weaves algebraic patterns just as the Jacquard loom weaves flowers and leaves'. Perhaps Samuel Butler was thinking of the Babbage machines when he declared (in *Erewhon*, 1872) that 'our sum-engines never drop a figure'.

A principal contribution of Babbage was that he identified what would become the main architectural components of the modern electronic digital computer.

Gulliver's Word-machine

This is the only fictional cameo in the book (apart from the speculative items in Chapter 14). It is worth citing because it shows remarkable prescience. There is a section in 'A Voyage to Laputa' (*Gulliver's Travels*), written by Jonathan Swift in 1726, in which a twenty-foot square frame for the automatic generation of books is described. The superficies were composed of pieces of wood, of different sizes and linked together by slender wires. Papers, on which were written all the words of a language ('in their several moods, tenses and declensions, but without any order'), were pasted to the bits of wood. From time to time the students took hold of the iron handles – there were forty set around the frame – and gave them a sudden turn, whereupon the dispositions of all the words changed. Some of the students would then read aloud the new sentences that had been randomly formed, and student scribes would take down the words. With many repetitions of the process, whole volumes were produced, the aim being 'out of those rich materials to give the world a complete body of all arts and sciences'. The scheme could be 'still improved and much expedited, if the public would raise a fund for making and employing five hundred such frames in Lagado . . .' Public funding, then as now, was an evident problem.

The Jaquet-Droz Automata

Pierre and Henri–Louis Jaquet-Droz constructed various automata in the eighteenth century. The Scribe (1770) and the Draughtsman (1772) are boys aged about three, and the Musician (1773) is a girl aged about sixteen. A complicated mechanism allows the girl to play a keyboard instrument, and another device operates a lever which causes the girl's chest to rise and fall in a perfect imitation of breathing. Other mechanisms cause her eyes and head to move: she can, for instance, move her eyes left and right, cast her eyes down, bend forward and straighten up. After she has played a melody, she performs a graceful bow. She, and other automata, currently inhabit the Musée d'Art et d'Histoire in Neuchâtel.

The Speaking Automaton

A speaking automaton, called Euphonia, was exhibited in the Egyptian Hall in Piccadilly in 1846. Professor Faber of Vienna spent twenty-five years constructing this device, an artificial bearded Turk designed to produce sounds similar to the human voice. Euphonia was able to recite the letters of the alphabet and then declare, 'How do you do, ladies and gentlemen?' It could also whisper, laugh and sing. Faber allowed people to inspect the device and they found that it contained a double bellows, keys and levers; its mouth moved and it had a tongue and an indiarubber palate. Since Euphonia was built in Austria, it spoke English with a German accent. People were said to be satisfied that no trickery was involved. Since the device was able to ask and answer questions – a complex feat, even for modern digital computers – it is difficult to see how the Turk could perform so well *without* trickery.

2. The Intelligent Machine

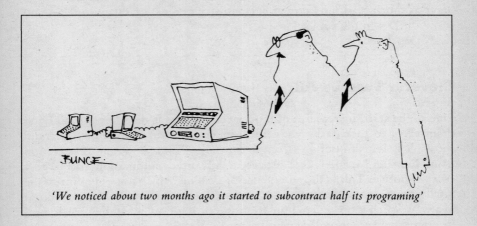

'We noticed about two months ago it started to subcontract half its programing'

Cleverer than Bertrand Russell?

No one will be surprised to hear that computers can do sums – some people seem to think that that is *all* they can do. And computers can also prove theorems. The Logic Theorist (written by Newell, Shaw and Simon in 1956), for instance, can prove theorems, and also solve a variety of other types of problems. This program was addressed to the logical theorems in Chapter 2 of *Principia Mathematica* (by Bertrand Russell and A. N. Whitehead): it not only succeeded in proving thirty-eight of the first fifty-two theorems in that seminal work, but also found at least one proof that Russell and Whitehead had missed! This achievement compares with the strides being made in the computer solution of chess problems (see 'Chess Computers Play', pp. 159–60).

As Clever as a Ph.D.?

Much publicity is now being given to computer-based expert systems. These fancy facilities can have conversations with human beings in specialist areas and give advice when necessary. Expert systems are now operating, with varying degrees of success, in such fields as geology, chemistry, medicine and engineering. Medical diagnostic systems (such as MYCIN) have been shown to be very successful, and one writer (Bernard Cole in *Interface Age*, April 1981) has observed that the expert systems DENDRAL and SECS 'have as much reasoning power in chemistry as most graduate students and some Ph.D.s in the subject'.

Cleverer Than Us All?

One of the startling features of modern computers is that they are applying themselves to their tasks with more ingenuity than human beings could show. It is worth quoting (from *Computing*, 17 July 1980) an observation from Donald Michie: 'One aspect of advanced automation has largely escaped notice. This is the emergence of systems which not only outrun the intellectual reach of those who are supposed to interact with them, but do so in a way which is opaque to human attempts to follow what they are doing.' In a remarkable chess performance, cited by Michie, the computer baffled the human chess experts: 'Nothing had prepared them for the bizarre strategies utilized by the system.' The point is that computers may not only be evolving superior intellects to all human beings, but that we will soon lose track of the high-level methods whereby the machines accomplish their tasks!

Anything You Can Do . . .

Some nervous folk take comfort in the thought that computers can only do what they're programmed to do – that they aren't capable of going beyond the specific intentions of their human programmers. Alas, such anxious observers will have to think again. Today, computers are even learning to program themselves – with results not always anticipated by the human programmers. For example, Ross Quinian (of the University of Sydney) has developed the ID3 system which is capable of 'automatic programming'. One of the system's accomplishments is to have written a chess-playing program which is about five times more efficient than the best program that the system's human master could produce. Quinian's program took 17.5 milliseconds to produce results on a large Cyber computer; but the ID3-generated program took only 3.4 milliseconds. It is this type of remarkable result that has caused Professor Donald Michie at Edinburgh

University to warn against allowing technology to lead society into a 'technological black hole' in which humans will no longer be able to understand the computer reasoning behind key decisions.

Computers as People

You will find in this book that children can treat computers as they might treat a pet puppy. We may find it more surprising that adults are learning to treat computers as if they were people. Two psychologists Karl E. Scheibe and Margaret Erwin, have investigated the tendency of subjects to react to a computer as if it were another person. Forty male and female undergraduates were asked to play computer games at a console. The computer intelligence was deliberately varied from one game to another, and there was always a tape-recorder present in the room. The human beings proved to be very vocal, with only one person not speaking at all! What was particularly interesting is that personal pronouns were often used to denote the computer. In all, 358 pronoun references were made, with the computer variously addressed as *it*, *he*, *you* and *they* – even as Fred! Perhaps surprisingly, the computer was never called *she* (the feminists can make what they want of this). The psychologists have cited examples of people who not only get angry with computers but accuse them of deliberate mischief. As computers become ever more intelligent and flexible in their behaviour, it will be increasingly easy to cast them in the role of persons.

The Barry Goldwater Machine

The 'machine' here is a program, not a lump of equipment. The idea behind the program is that Barry Goldwater's clear-headed (or simple-minded) beliefs can be nicely encapsulated in the sorts of definitions and sequences that computer operations require. R. P. Abelson wrote the program to mimic the then presidential candidate. It included facile references to the 'God-fearing Americans' and to their evil opponents, the 'Communists and their liberal dupes'. This entertaining program has passed into the folklore of artificial intelligence (AI). Those who disagree with Goldwater and his ilk may like to consider the program an agreeable example of artificial *un*intelligence.

The Tony Benn Machine

Some people may have suspected that Tony Benn was computerized. Adrian Berry (author of *The Super-Intelligent Machine*, 1983), intrigued by Abelson's Barry Goldwater Machine, decided to write a Tony Benn program – because his ideology (as expressed in his speeches) is 'relatively clear and self-consistent'. When the program starts to run a message appears on the screen: 'HI, I'M TONY BENN, WHAT SHALL WE TALK ABOUT?' The operator then selects a subject from five that are listed beneath the question. Having chosen 'Parliament', Berry had the following exchange (the computer's remarks in capitals):

> THE HOUSE OF LORDS IS A PARASITIC INSTITUTION. COMRADES, LET US CAMPAIGN FOR ITS ABOLITION. LET US BREAK DOWN THOSE GILDED DOORS, AND LET THE FREE LIGHT OF PARLIAMENTARY DEMOCRACY SHINE THROUGH THEM.

> Don't you see a danger that a one-chamber government could lead to a dictatorship?

> DICTATORSHIP? THAT'S A GOOD QUESTION AND I'M GLAD YOU ASKED IT. THE ANSWER IS PERFECTLY CLEAR, AS I'VE MADE CLEAR IN NUMEROUS SPEECHES . . .

This is an engaging exercise (though we may feel that it reveals more of Adrian Berry's political proclivities than of Tony Benn's ideology). Twenty-four 'Socialist outbursts' are programmed into the system, though it is conceded that 'by no effort of imagination could anyone suppose that there was a real politician inside the machine'.

Chips Designing Chips

One problem about the designing of silicon chips – out of which nearly all modern computers are made (some are made of something else, like gallium arsenide) – is that chip design is becoming too complicated for mere human beings to cope with. So computers (that is, chips) have to come to the rescue. One particular design task, the laying out of electronic circuits, can be particularly time-consuming – and this is one place where computers can help. Today, many chip designers use computer programs that lay out a chip pattern automatically. It is still necessary for human designers to cooperate with the computer designer at various stages but, progressively and inevitably, the circle is being closed: Increasingly, chips are performing the necessary design tasks, just as, in another context, programs are writing programs. This type of phenomenon may variously be seen as incestuous or self-reproductive. It is obvious that computers are increasingly intervening to influence the direction of their own evolution. Man is not yet squeezed out of the process. Not yet . . .

Robot Computer Brains

The need for robots to have their own brains has been met by developments in modern microelectronics. In the past, the robot brain could be contained in a separate room and linked to the robot torso by means of cables: there are obvious disadvantages to this arrangement, not least that robot mobility is severely restricted. Today efforts are being made to provide 'on–board' brains for robots, so that effective intelligence is provided where it is needed. And this also means that expensive factory floor-space can be occupied by robots rather than by computers. In a typical application, an on–board computer is required to control up to six robot axis motors in real time (torso, shoulder, elbow, wrist pitch and roll, and optional hand and gripper). The task of providing an on–board robot brain has been tackled by International Robomation/Intelligence, for example, by putting no less than eight microprocessors on a printed circuit board. These provide enough 'computer horsepower' to give the robot an effective intelligence.

The Peg-inserting Robot

It seems a simple enough thing to do, to hold a peg, locate a hole and insert the peg in the hole. But robots have problems accomplishing even this much. They are apt to 'cross–lock' the peg, managing to jam it in various ways. One solution is to equip the hand with a range of sensors. With a sense of touch, the robot can detect the resistances to the peg entering the hole, and then take suitable action to reduce the resistances to zero. This generally entails moving the peg about until its path is clear. Another solution to this problem has been found by the Charles Stark Draper Laboratory in the United States. It has long been known that a *pulled* peg is more likely to locate in a hole than a *pushed* peg. A clever device, using the notion of 'compliance', can make a pushed peg behave as if it were being pulled: resistance to the peg motion is detected and a new alignment is attempted. The development of the compliance device – called the Remote Centre Compliance (RCC) – all goes to show how difficult it is to get robots to do even the tasks that most human beings find extremely simple.

Robots with Sensitive Skin

When someone touches our skin we generally notice, and we have tended to assume that this capacity distinguishes us from machines – but not any more! Today technology is developing ways of making robots 'know' when they are touched – when, for example, they have to manipulate an object or when they inadvertently come into contact with an object in their vicinity. A remarkable 'artificial skin' sensor has been developed by the Laboratoire d'Automatique et d'Analyse des Systèmes in Toulouse, and already this skin sensor has been able to identify the position of a mechanical part with multiple planar equilibrium faces. Artificial 'skin' of this sort has been incorporated into a robot gripper to help the robot sense items during grasping. The sensitive skin consists of a printed-circuit board on which there are a number of receptive spots, like nerve endings. A small voltage is applied to a guard ring around the spots, and the electrical characteristics of a conductive coating on the structure vary according to the pressure exerted. At every test spot, there is a variation in the current which can be analysed to indicate the shape of an object being touched by the sensor. The resulting information pattern can be analysed by computer. Now robots can recognize what they are handling.

The Computerized Sense of Touch

Researchers at the Carnegie-Mellon University and the California Institute of Technology have developed an effective touch sensor for robots. This device incorporates a special computing circuit as part of the sensor itself: an applied force can be sensed, analysed and transmitted over a link to cause appropriate robot action. Many earlier conductive plastic sensors have used passive substrates to carry electrodes, but this device exploits the surface characteristics of a silicon chip. Put simply, a robot hand can be given intelligence! This can make for a more rapid robot response and more effective robot behaviour. With such an approach it is easy to see how working intelligence could be distributed throughout the body of a robot. Dinosaurs may have had two brains: robots can have dozens, variously concerned with movement, sensing, thought, etc.

The Robot's Feeling Fingers

Robot fingers are being developed in many research laboratories. At GEC-Marconi, for instance, existing robots are being modified to make them able to carry out a wide range of activities formerly the sole province of dexterous human beings. One tack is to develop sensitive robot fingers that could be used to assemble delicate electronic assemblies. One current robot gripper has four fingers which are able to hold small parts such as integrated circuits. It is suggested that later robots could have as many as sixteen fingers. The fingered robots could be used to insert silicon chips on to printed-circuit boards, a task that people do at present. To be that skilful, a robot must be able to repeat movements with an accuracy of not more than 0.1 mm, and it must be fast. A person can build a printed-circuit board with about fifty parts in about five minutes. Even the best robots in the early 1980s are three to ten times too slow. Robots, like computers, do not always outperform human beings.

The Brain-in-leg Robot

Part of the fascination of modern robots is that they are becoming mobile – though they still don't move very quickly. For an automaton, walking is a highly complex task, and computer control is essential. Here the computer is required to regulate a machine's gait, to prevent the machine from tipping over, to distribute lateral forces among the legs, to make sure that the legs are not driven past their limit of travel, to choose places for stepping that will provide adequate support, etc. These can represent difficult computational tasks, and various strategies are being developed to overcome them. For example, some six-legged robots do not need to balance, and on-board microcomputers can handle the remaining computational needs. Four-legged robots, hopping robots and other mobile systems are also being developed. The day is past when robots have to spend their days shackled to a factory floor or in the corner of a research laboratory. Soon they will be more mobile than many a sedentary office worker!

The Better to See You With

Science fiction has always been full of robots with powerful limbs and dauntingly effective senses. By the early 1980s it was manifestly obvious that technology was rapidly translating fiction into fact. Computers were, for instance, developing their own eyes (at least one caption under a picture of a sighted robot runs: 'Watch what you're doing, mate!'). In nature, there are many different types of eyes: think of insects, spiders, flatfish and human beings. Computers are learning to develop a similar diversity. One technique, developed by a French Government unit near Paris, is to use laser range-finders which can translate information about the shape of objects into data that a computer can store. An object is placed on a swivel table illuminated by a laser. Cameras move to focus on the spot of light produced by the beam, and a computer uses trigonometry to work out the position of the spot of light, and hence the position of the part of the object being illuminated. The computer then moves the position of the spot and a new computation can take place. The results of each computation are stored in the computer memory, allowing a picture of the object's shape to be progressively constructed. The more powerful the computer, the more rapidly it can 'see' the shape of an object – or of you!

A Computer to Recognize You

The Wisard computer-based pattern-recognition system being developed at Brunel University will be able to recognize the human face. In this type of application, 512 by 512 picture-points representing a human face can be tested for correspondence with stored images. Handprints and other patterns can also be recognized. What is particularly interesting is that Wisard can be *taught* to recognize particular faces: once taught, it can recognize a face in less than three seconds – a skill that could be of use in security and other applications.

Robot Vision in Use

The earliest robots were simple 'pick-and-place' devices, designed to collect and transfer items from one defined spot to another. This has always been a necessary type of activity in a factory environment, but the simple robots had little skill: parts had to be correctly positioned and of the right shape, otherwise the robot would get confused and be unable to function efficiently. Today, robots are more intelligent and increasingly able to cope with variations and unpredictable events in their workplace. For instance, Objection Recognition Systems of Princeton has recently introduced an industrial robot, the 'i-bot 1', that can retrieve parts that are jumbled randomly in a box or bin. The robot is provided with a sight capability by means of a camera mounted seven feet above the work area. The arm is computer-controlled and can adjust its behaviour to the increasing depth of the parts in the bin as items are removed. The robot can be trained to recognize objects, after which it can function independently, using its eye to check what it is doing!

Watching the Walking Person

In general, if a machine can 'see', it must know something about the item it is looking at. This means that artificial vision systems are often provided with *general* information about the objects they are likely to encounter. An alternative approach is to give the system *specific* knowledge about the items it is expected to see in its environment. The WALKER computer program is an example of this second approach, and it has been described as 'a program to see a walking person'. The program maps images into a description in which a person is portrayed by a series of hierarchical levels – that is, as having an arm, which has a lower-arm, which has a hand, for instance. A machine-generated picture can be superimposed over original photographic images. This highly sophisticated system was conditioned by a number of constraints relating to position, movement and posture. The WALKER program has been tested in various ways. It tends to assume that a walker is present in the scene and then works to find it. If there are several walkers in the picture, or if there are none at all, the program becomes confused. Sometimes computers do not seem particularly bright!

Computers to Read Newspapers

We now have programs that can be used to summarize newspaper articles, though with rather unimpressive accuracy. For instance, the Frump program from Yale University refers a text to one of its forty-eight 'sketchy scripts' – sets of rules under general headings such as 'disaster', 'fighting', 'arrest' and 'demonstration'. Frump is likely to understand a simple factual story, but does less well when the texts include humour, sentiment or metaphor. This is one text that Frump handled well:

> Santiago (UPI) – The Chilean Government has seized operational and financial control of the U.S. interest in the El Teniente Mining Company, one of the three big copper enterprises here . . .

It took Frump just 3.46 seconds to conclude that 'CHILE HAS NATIONALIZED AN AMERICAN MINE'. More worryingly, it was mystified by the following report:

> Moscow (UPI) – Soviet President Leonid Brezhnev told a group of visiting U.S. Senators on Friday that the Soviet Union had once 'tested but never started production of' a neutron bomb. But one Senator said he did not consider the statement 'a serious matter'.

In 7.9 seconds, Frump decided that 'RUSSIAN BOMBERS HAVE ATTACKED RUSSIA'. When Frump was subsequently told that testing a bomb was not necessarily a hostile act, the program correctly concluded that 'LEONID BREZHNEV TOLD THE UNITED STATES THAT RUSSIA HAD TESTED A BOMB'.

A Robot to 'See' Smells

There is now a chemical-based robot visual-guidance system for use in a range of industrial applications. A test was performed by the Optical Engineering Group of the University of Dayton (Ohio) Research Institute to show that a new optical scanner could react to chemical compounds in components and tools. This device suggests the startling ramification that robots will soon be able to respond to industrial tools and components without needing outside programming. More generally, this is yet another indication of how robots are evolving senses unknown in the biological world.

Smelling Those Poisonous Gases

We are learning not to be surprised at the fact that robots are sprouting limbs and computer brains and developing a range of effective senses to help them to function in the real world. We encounter various instances of computer 'eyes' in the present book, and we find the occasional ear. Computers, we now see, are developing sensitive noses! A sense of smell is obviously useful to human beings and to other animals. We would expect computers to want one as well. It can be very helpful if smell sensors are linked to computer facilities to provide adequate warning of toxic gases in the environment – gases that are poisonous to human beings (computers are not yet troubled by such things). One technique is to exploit the conductivity of a semiconducting material. Such materials have long been known to be affected by the presence of certain gases in the atmosphere. The typical reactions in the semiconductor are reversible: the substances can detect a toxic gas and then revert to normal so that it can work again and again. Put in a nutshell, smell sensors of this type exploit the reversible chemisorption of gases with a resulting change of conductivity proportional to the gas concentration. Semiconductors have been developed to recognize specific gases, so there may be a foul smell in the air to which the sensitive computer nose is totally oblivious!

Computers to Understand Images

There is often a requirement – in industry or domestic entertainment, for example – to convert video images into useful information. Now computers are being given the job. Such a development can find many uses, from equipping robots with eyes to making it possible to analyse parts of the human body for medical and other purposes. In one system – a Linear Array Processor promoted by British Robotic Systems in conjunction with the

National Physical Laboratory – a network of microprocessors is used to analyse picture elements of an image received from a TV camera. The machine should speed up the operation of British Robotic System's key product, the Viking vision unit (an artificial 'seeing' system). Viking can, for example, check the design of postage stamps, and feed shape information to a robot to enable the robot gripper to pick up the item in question. Other computers analysing visual data are beginning to understand patterns of blood vessels in tissue and to appreciate the disposition of components in jaw-bones. One computer-based system, at the Imperial Cancer Research Fund, is investigating the structure of proteins.

Robots are Getting Hungry

No robot or computer can work without an adequate supply of energy: in short, we have to feed the beasts. Sometimes they are even able to tell us when they are hungry, and to do something about it. Don't worry: so far their culinary taste does not extend beyond electricity. One pleasant example of a hungry robot is the machine developed by Dr Alan Bond at the Artificial Intelligence Unit of London University. The robot runs off a battery whose power level is characterized by one of four codes – *full charge*, *hungry*, *low* and *very low*. When the battery power drops to 'hungry', the robot grows concerned and starts searching for a special charging-point in the laboratory. As it searches, it emits a hungry crying sound which may upset its human observers. The area around the recharging point is painted a combination of different colours which the robot can recognize. One idea is that in due course the robot will be able to work out the connection between a light over the recharging point and its hungry code. In short, some robots are learning to detect when their stomachs are empty and how to fill them.

Who Said That?

Just as computers can recognize human faces, so they can recognize human voices; they can tell one voice from another for security and other purposes. Sadaoki Furui, working at Bell Laboratories, has been interested in developing computers to the point when they can identify an individual's voice-pattern. So the computer may know *who* is talking but may not –

unless it also has a voice-understanding facility – have a clue *what* is being said. The Furui system requires each speaker to build up a personal reference file by telephoning the computer and saying a test phrase – one that the computer is skilled at analysing. The telephone signals are digitized and held as a spectrum of 'peaks' and 'valleys'. The computer is then able to measure time variations in the spectral features and to transform the data to show voice-characteristics as a function of time. The next time the speaker talks to the computer on the telephone line, the computer compares the voice with what is held in the reference file. In one experiment, the computer achieved a 99 per cent success rate in identifying speakers – even when imposters tried to imitate voices!

The Glaswegian Robot

We tend to think that voice-recognition robots can only understand words spoken to them in standard English (or standard Japanese). Now things are changing fast. At the Automan '83 exhibition, a robot on show had been taught to respond to commands given with a heavy Glaswegian accent, a far remove from standard English. The robot has other capabilities as well. It can, for instance, etch initials on glass paperweights, a trick it happily performed at the Cincinnati Milacron stand. Scotsman Andrew Mackie, an employee of CAP Reading, taught the robot the alphabet after linking the device to an Intel 8086 microprocessor. The overall system is controlled by a version of Intel's 570 speech transaction development set. The robot is said to be able to remember up to three thousand points in six axes of motion. The robot has demonstrated its powers of comprehension by pointing, on command, to the letters of the alphabet drawn on a blackboard.

The Obedient Robot

Robots are of little use if they don't do what you tell them; one of the advantages of voice recognition is that the human issuing of orders takes on a familiar character. Robots can, of course, be instructed by tape or an on-board silicon-chip program. But it is nice to be able to talk to the fellows. Dr David Bourne does this at Carnegie-Mellon University using a microcomputer and a voice-input system. He issues commands and the robot obeys. Bourne says, 'Getting the robot to follow orders was not the impossible task a lot of people would have had us believe. One of the engineers on staff here sat down with me and in about ten hours we had what we needed.' This particular functional robot is little more than an animated arm, but it can recognize a series of one-word commands. If, for example, you say 'Up', the robot will raise its arm. Dr Bourne has commented: 'What we're coming up with is pretty exciting.'

Robots with All the Senses

A robot may have 'eyes', 'ears' or a sensitive 'nose'. Some robots, with sensitive skin or other facilities, have an effective sense of touch. A few robots have more than one sense – and may include senses that are not known in human beings (for example, ultrasonic range-finding, magnetic sensitivity, etc.). Increasingly, thought is being given to equipping robots with a *range* of senses, so that they can operate with maximum flexibility in their world. Work in Japan (for instance, at the Tokyo Institute of Technology) is focusing on providing robots with integrated systems to allow a range of artificial senses to cooperate for maximum effect. One paper (in *Sensor Review*, January 1982) considers how various tactile (touch), proximity and visual sensors could be linked in an overall system. The aim is an efficient *total sensor system*. And there is great flexibility in this approach. For example, there are provisions for hard touch, soft touch and reflex touch (with this latter, the artificial finger withdraws after touch), and grasp may vary in power and duration. The advantages of a total sensor system are many. Particular senses may be better than others in particular circumstances; and one sense may be used to corroborate the findings of others. The multi-sensed robot is already with us. Soon the beasts will have more senses than we do!

The Reading/Speaking Computer

If you ever grow tired of reading to the kids at bedtime, then you may like the idea of a computer that can scan the printed page and then speak the words it sees. Two Finnish researchers have been working to develop a machine that can translate text into speech for the benefit of blind and dumb people. Matti

Karjalainen and Unto Laine of the State Research Centre in Tampere have produced prototypes of a speaking machine in which speech is synthesized by a computer with word input via a keyboard. And they have also developed a device for translating the printed page into spoken words. One problem is that the machine has been programmed to cope with Finnish, a language notorious for its complex structure but one that is easy to phoneticize. The Helsinki School for the Blind has been experimenting with one of the machines. A commercially acceptable story reader – for blind people or bedtime children – may, however, be some way off.

The Talking Typewriter

Two scientists, Peter Hall and Richard Rogers at the University of Tasmania (Hobart), have developed a talking computer to help blind typists. This clever system comprises an Osborne I micro, an Olivetti electronic typewriter, and a Votrax synthesizer board. The operator can tell the system to speak out any line, word or paragraph. One aim is to make it easy for blind typists to proof-read and correct textual errors. It is also hoped, by the Tasmanian charity marketing the product, that local paraplegics will be able to assemble the talking-typewriter system.

Spelling by Silicon Chip

What's your spelling like? Some educationalists may incline to think that it doesn't matter too much if you inadvertently transpose an i and an e, or double up a letter when you shouldn't. For those of us who want to spell as well as we can, there is at least one computer system to help. The WORD Plus facility, made available by the US firm Software Distributors, can proof-read text at the rate of five thousand words a minute, looking up the correct spellings, and making the necessary alterations. And to follow this, it can count the words if you want it to, and solve anagrams and crosswords. What will pedantic teachers say about this one?

Your (Computerized) Master's Voice

One consequence of computerized private telephone exchanges is that human beings are less sure about how to use them – so the computer will tell them how to proceed. In a new IBM system, a minicomputer acts as a vast telephone-answering machine, with room for as many as seven hundred 'guidance messages' in a choice of five languages. The Audio Distribution System is able to store digitized messages on magnetic disks and to relay them at some future time. Callers can leave messages with the system, and also collect messages left for them. Users of the system can add extra comments to a message before passing it on to a third party, or the computer can be instructed to send out messages on particular days. The system can even 'slim down' messages by cutting out long unnecessary pauses, though it cannot yet dispense with 'ums' and 'ers'. The computer, recognizing that mere human beings may have difficulty mastering the operational intricacies, is quite prepared to instruct people how to use it. If you are thinking of installing one of the systems at home, it currently costs around £100,000.

Computers to Understand Chinese

Natural language – English, French, Russian, Japanese and so on – is often, from a computer point of view, seen as vague and irrational. Where there is an immense number of characters in a language, as in Chinese, the computer has a colossal comprehension task on its hands: semantics and syntax, often inconsistent and ambiguous, are bad enough, but a vast character scheme is doubly unhelpful. In 1979 the British printing company Monotype sold its laser-printing method of computerizing the Chinese language to book publishing houses in Peking and Shanghai. Furthermore, the company has developed methods for typesetting Chinese newspapers. The Chinese printers initially wanted no less than 60,000 characters available in the computerized system, but a politically stimulated compromise resulted in 8,000 characters immediately available on line, with another 15,000 characters available on storage. Where Chinese printers have relied on manual methods, the number of characters is such that printers literally roller-skate along rows of cabinets holding the pieces of type! Perhaps computers will be able to cut down on the need for roller-skates.

The Computer Translator

Just as computers can work with newspaper texts, correct spellings, generate textual summaries and analyse source material to determine authorship, so they can translate from one language to another. This has, however, proved to be an immensely problematic area of computer application. The main difficulty is the complexity of human language. Comprehension of terms, for example, often depends upon a vast and shifting body of knowledge, which is difficult to build into computer systems. Moreover, human syntax and semantics often lack consistency, and computers have not yet learned to handle inconsistencies, 'fuzziness', and vague categories with aplomb. But the situation is changing (machine translation is a central aim of the current fifth-generation research programme in Japan). It is reckoned that today there are already more than twenty effective machine-translation systems in regular use around the world.

Teaching the Computer Translator

We know that, for various reasons, computers have difficulty translating from one human language to another. At Brigham Young University, people have been asked to 'converse' with a computer to aid the initial analysis of language. This approach is helping the computer to make sense – in terms of both syntax and semantics – of what it is translating. The Utah system is based on a language-structure model developed in the 1960s and known as junction grammar (JG). In JG, the meaning of a sentence can be computed from the relationships between the individual meanings of identifiable 'nodes'. This type of analysis accommodates both syntax and meaning. A person tells the computer which meaning to adopt in a particular context, whereupon the machine analyses and records relevant information and stores it for future reference. In this way the source text can be translated into a number of 'target' languages. At Utah, researchers have adopted this approach to allow the computer to translate from English into Spanish, Portuguese, German, French and Chinese. It is thought that, in due course, the computer will be able to translate with little or no human assistance.

The Multilingual Watch

The businessman or tourist in foreign lands doesn't need a phrasebook any more. Now he can use the multi-language wrist-watch dictionary from Casio. This remarkable device provides the traveller with an electronic phrasebook of thirty-six basic sentences in five languages, including French, German and Japanese. And there is also an English–Spanish dictionary of 1,711 words. Words and phrases can be found by using buttons to search through the listings alphabetically. If you are worried about reading Japanese, the words are shown phonetically in Roman characters, not in Japanese ideograms. The watch can also be used for telling the time!

The Deep-sea Speech Improver

It has been known for a long time that distortion can often bedevil the speech from deep-sea divers. Some years ago, a lecturer at Edinburgh University designed a device using silicon chips to unscramble the distorted speech. The distortions are caused by the helium–oxygen mixture that divers have to breathe, and bulky unscrambling equipment has traditionally been necessary before divers could talk to other divers or to people on the surface. Dr Mervyn Jack built a compact unscrambler which, in due course, will be no larger than a matchbox. The system maintains a high quality of speech reproduction. Thus if the life-line of a diver is cut, it is now possible for the diver to stay in contact using a chip-controlled radio.

The Promotional Robot

In this commercial world, it is inevitable that robots would be drafted to sell things. One promotional robot touring America before 1980 was Orion, who was quite capable of approaching a girl to ask for a kiss or a dance. When a female gives Orion a kiss on the dome, his antenna shoots up and spins uncontrollably. If a girl agrees to dance, then Orion helpfully switches on one of his tapes. When people don't talk to Orion, he asks them why they don't like him. But sometimes Orion can be malicious: on one occasion he asked a man for his tie and then fed it through a shredding machine. But the robot doesn't always have things his way. At a commercial show in New York, a woman attacked Orion, finally pushing him down a flight of stairs. The robot finished his appearance with one broken arm in a sling. By 1980, Orion had amused and annoyed people in more than forty states of the US. Terry Palmer, 'father' of Orion, has said: 'He's like a son to me. The first day our daughter went to school, she told her teacher she had a robot for a brother. The next day I had to take Orion in for the teacher and the class to see.'

The Sales Promotional Androids

Promotional robots come in various shapes and sizes. By the late 1970s, Quasar Industries had three dozen such creatures, which the company liked to call Sales Promotional Androids (SPAs). In addition, the company has manufactured a domestic robot servant, a seven-foot high security-guard robot, and a robot to work in hospitals. The SPAs are five feet four inches tall, a size that was selected according to psychological principles for maximum appeal at promotional events. The typical SPA runs on hidden tyres (up to a speed of twenty miles per hour), and has independently programmed arms, elbows and hands. One SPA is reported as curing a sick child: the boy, in shock after a car accident, refused to talk, but was soon chattering away when left with the robot. And when the prototype for the domestic robot was brought to Britain there were a number of interesting events. The robot bought his own ticket at the airport, and later took over from the stewardess on the aircraft to serve breakfast ('. . . it began going up and down the aisle serving grapefruit to passengers that morning.').

The Water-pouring Robot

Many modern robots are skilled enough to pour water from one container to another. WABOT-1 is a famous experimental robot that can do this and many other things. Described as an 'information-powered machine', it has senses and limbs, and can analyse circumstances of the environment to facilitate decision-making. By any account, it seems a pretty intelligent fellow. WABOT-1 was built at Waseda University in Tokyo: its hands carry touch sensors, and it is also equipped with sight and hearing. You can tell WABOT-1 to find a cylinder in the room, whereupon it first acknowledges the command verbally. Then its eye scans the environment until the item is located. The robot works out how far it is to proceed, and then sets off. Half-way there, it stops to check its data. Finally it moves to pick the cylinder up and transport it to the correct destination. WABOT-1 has been depicted as a 'human-type hydraulic walking machine'.

The Block-moving Robot

In 1968 the Stanford Research Institute first introduced the Shakey robot to the world. The first version of Shakey was equipped with a television camera (to give the machine sight), an optical range-finder and bump detectors. Shakey, dubbed 'the first complete robot system', moved on wheels and was particularly skilled at assembling blocks and moving them from one room to another. In 1971, Shakey was rebuilt and required to perform a range of additional tasks. Not only was he required to play with his blocks, but he was obliged to negotiate a ramp, push blocks off the edge, and open doors. Perhaps most interestingly, he was required to cooperate with another robot, a Unimate manipulator. This is really a fascinating development. You will find in these pages at least one other example of cooperating machines. Perhaps robots and computers are developing a social sense!

Rubik Cubot

A group of twenty scientists from Battelle's Pacific North-west Laboratories have built a robot, called Cubot, to solve Rubik's Cube. There are now many computer programs for this purpose, appearing, for instance, in a wide range of personal-computer journals. What is remarkable about the new robot is that it does not need to borrow human fingers! Cubot, using its own metallic fingers, camera eye and computer brain, can solve any scrambled Rubik's Cube in less than four minutes! Think of it: you mix up the Cube, give it to the robot, and wait for the performance. Cubot *looks at* the disposition of the cube elements, *decides* on a course of action, and then *cleverly manipulates* the elements until the solution is achieved! Are there still people around who doubt that computers are intelligent?

The Imaginary Rubik Cube

Today many computer programs exist for the purpose of solving the Rubik Cube, and many of the programs are for microcomputers (it may be thought that the large 'mainframes' are too class-conscious to bother with such trivia). One computer buff, Jim Hodsdon, has programmed his 'poor unsuspecting H8 computer to simulate a Rubik Cube'. What this means, in effect, is that the computer imagines a Cube, and then proceeds to solve it in its head! Could you do that trick? In this particular case, the program is written in Benton Harbor Extended Basic and comprises more than seven hundred lines. This program, dubbed 'Autosolve', will unscramble any scrambled Rubik Cube . . . without ever seeing a Cube. Just tell the computer where the Cube's component elements are, and Autosolve will do its job.

The Osaka Robot

The Osaka Demonstration Robot, displayed at Expo '70, was able to perform many feats, including moving around and carrying people! The robot comprises a head, a large body (capable of rising to a height of twenty-four feet), a base, and two arms of different lengths. Two control rooms are located in the head, one of which causes the robot to respond to received information by producing smoke, smells, light and sounds. When the body is raised to its maximum position, the base becomes a stage and the robot can then perform a wide range of different movements.

The Friendly Grey Computer

This fellow – full name, The Friendly Grey Computer (Star Gauge Model 54) – was built in 1965 out of fibreglass, paint, electronic components, doll parts and a rocking chair, and currently lives in the Museum of Modern Art, New York. As you may have guessed, this robot is a tongue-in-cheek contraption, built to exemplify a few modern (for 1965) computer principles but with very little that is very serious in mind. The brief *directions for operation* include the observations, 'Computers sometimes get fatigued and have nervous breakdowns, hence the chair for it to rest in. If you know your computer

well, you can tell when it's tired and sort of blue and in a funky mood.'
However, once the rocker switch has been left on for ten or twenty minutes,
things will improve ('Your computer will love it and work all the harder for
you.').

The Computer Booby-trap

No, this isn't a standard booby-trap linked to a computer for some purpose.
It is an altogether different creature. Some software companies have taken to
putting peculiar facilities in their programs – like extra lines of code that will
disable the program if bills are not paid on time. This remarkable way of
collecting debts relies on the fact that most computers contain clocks to
record the passage of the weeks, months and years. A program routine –
about which the customer may be totally unaware – can be arranged to check
the date on the clock before the main section of the program is allowed to
proceed. Nor is it easy to find the booby-trap (or 'time-bomb', as one
journalist dubbed it): few programmers would want to wade through the
reams of code to find the booby-trap. In one celebrated case, a man was
accused at Chelmsford crown court of deliberately inserting such a routine
into a software package for motor dealers that his company was developing
for another software firm. The result was that, after a set date, all the data in a
Systime computer was corrupted. The jury could not decide on a verdict.
Take care: who knows what is lurking in your software?

A New Intelligence Ingredient

Artificial intelligence has many aspects. We may need a powerful computer
with massive storage or fancy pieces of software – to carry out the tasks that
in a human being would be seen as intelligent. Or we may need better
computer languages (current AI research tends to favour such languages as
Lisp and Prolog). Recently a new language – appropriately called the Artificial
Intelligence Language – has been announced. This language could make it
easier for human beings to interact with computers. There would be no need
to learn a difficult 'high-level' computer language. The idea is that untrained
users could scan through a database posing questions in ordinary English,
rather than in the forced statements that most database systems seem to

require. The Artificial Intelligence Language exploits aspects of pattern recognition, and also enables the computer to parse the sentences, deciding which words are verbs, nouns, adverbs, etc. It is thought that the new language could make it easier to exploit the potential of computers in such areas as housing, hospitals, law and order, and social security.

Programs to Write Programs

We have seen that computers can write their own programs. This startling development suggests that even computer programmers may one day become redundant. It is worth giving another instance of this type of trick. The *program-generator*, an increasingly common software animal, is now emerging in various shapes and sizes. Some programs can write programs for untutored users; some can create a tailor-made program for the initiate. We are seeing, for example, a number of programs that can help people to write code in the language Basic. Program-generators have been used for some years with large computers; today they are becoming available for micros. Typical programs that help you to write Basic for a microcomputer are Autocode, Codewriter and The Last One. We may speculate on what the emergence of program-generators really signifies. Some pessimists may claim that this development represents a progressive accumulation of programming expertise in computer systems, while at the same time human specialists become less and less necessary. Computers develop their competence, while people are discouraged from acquiring any! Optimists may see program-generators as *aids* and nothing more, much in the way that they regard 'expert systems' as tools, not as experts.

3. Science and Research

'Sooner or later, Clive, someone is going to find out.'

The Computer Mathematician

There is a sense in which all computers have mathematical competence, but not all systems can carry out the sophisticated computations needed by scientists and engineers. MACSYMA, originally designed in the United States in 1968, is a vast computer system used to assist mathematicians, scientists and engineers in tackling mathematical problems. The system, still growing, includes a large numerical subroutine library. Today,

MACSYMA, running on a DEC KL–10 at MIT and accessed through the ARPA network, is used by hundreds of US researchers. Workers from government laboratories, universities and private companies spend much of every day logged into the system. As with most other expert systems, the performance of MACSYMA depends upon an extensive knowledge base, allowing the interactive system to perform more than six hundred different types of mathematical operations – including differentiation, integration, equation solving, matrix operations and vector algebra. MACSYMA currently comprises about 230,000 words of program code (in the Lisp language), and further code is available, written in MACSYMA's own programming language. MACSYMA is evolving as new mathematical techniques are added to the system. Already it has a mathematical competence that far outstrips that of any human being.

Hunting the Biggest Prime

Computers, as we may expect, are very good at hunting for particular numbers. In 1983 it was reported that computers working for several months had discovered the largest ever prime number (a prime number is a whole number which, apart from fractions, can only be divided by the numbers 1 and itself). It is impractical to write this number down in the normal way. If printed in a newspaper like the *Guardian*, it would occupy no less than three and a half pages! It is more tamely expressed as $2^{86243}-1$, which means that you multiply 2 by itself 86,243 times and then subtract 1. The resulting number has 25,962 digits. If you want to check this using a pencil and paper, it will probably take you several years. It took the Cray-1 machine, the most powerful computer in the world, 1 hour, 3 minutes and 22 seconds to check that the new number was truly a prime. I feel inclined not to argue.

The Computer Psychologist

We know that computers can be interested in such topics as neurosis and paranoia. Now, at little cost, they are willing to assess your personality. The 'Bipolar Psychological Inventory' is a program represented as a multi-dimensional personality test. It administers, scores and interprets tests, and prints out comments about your mental equipment. If you do not like what it says, you can try lying to it. The computer – an Apple II, for instance – will probably not notice. This psychology program costs around £100, and it's not much use without a computer. Perhaps when the system has insulted *you*, you can invite it to submit its own personality traits for analysis.

Weighing an Animal

Weighing a dead animal is easy, as is weighing an unconscious animal; the accurate weighing of a live animal that is apt to wriggle or jump about can be difficult. But this requirement has occupied the minds of zoologists carrying out weight-loss experiments. Now, computer-based instruments manufactured by Sartorius Instruments (based in West Germany) can help. The use of a small computer makes it easy to find the weight of a small animal inclined to wriggle around and upset ordinary balances. A microprocessor is programmed to take a sample of weight readings over a period – to take into account the split seconds when the animal is not actually touching the weighing pan. The readings are integrated over time, and an average figure is flashed on to a display window to indicate the animal's correct weight.

Understanding Dolphins

If human beings cannot understand dolphins, then maybe computers can. Scientists at the Institute for Delphinid Research (IDR) in Grassy Key, Florida, are now using an Apple II microcomputer, with a 'listener board' and a modified Mountain Computer Music System, to overcome one of the major difficulties in dolphin communication research: the different frequency ranges of human and dolphin hearing and 'speaking'. Bottlenose dolphins can use a very broad range of frequencies: from about 2,000 to 150,000 cycles per second. This compares with human speech that generally ranges from 150 to 3,000 cycles per second (though most people can hear frequencies of up to 20,000 cycles per second). Thus many of the sounds made by each species are inaudible to the other. The new computer-based system can translate human whistles into signals well within the dolphin's hearing range, and dolphin whistles can be brought down into the human hearing range. Already dolphins have been taught nouns (such as body parts and objects) and actions (such as 'jump', 'hold' and 'touch'). Now, with the aid of a computer, we may expect such work to accelerate.

The Imaginary Ice-sheet

Computers can now imagine what a Pleistocene ice-sheet was like. David Sugden of Aberdeen University has developed a computerized model of the Laurentide ice-sheet that covered Eastern North America several times during the Pleistocene period. This makes it possible for the computer to reconstruct the physical properties of the vanished ice-sheet. In particular it is possible to arrive at a value of the thermal properties at the base of the ice-sheet, a factor of critical importance in understanding the nature of regional glacial landscapes. This remarkable accomplishment – in effect, enabling a computer to 'imagine' in detail a long-disappeared ice-sheet – will enlarge our understanding of glacial zones throughout the world.

Computerized Chemical Analysis and Synthesis

Artificial intelligence methods have been applied to a variety of non-numeric chemical reasoning problems. This has led to effective computer-based systems for identifying molecular structures in unknown organic compounds, and for planning a sequence of reactions to synthesize organic chemical compounds. The identification of molecular structures is crucial to a wide range of problems in chemistry, biology and medicine; and this task is now being tackled by such expert systems as DENDRAL, CONGEN, Meta-DENDRAL and CRYSALIS. Meta-DENDRAL, for example, is able to infer the rules of mass spectrometry from examples of molecular structures already analysed by human beings; and DENDRAL has determined the structures of many types of molecules (such as marine sterols, antibiotics and insect pheromones). By contrast, such expert systems as LHASA, SECS and SYNCHEM are concerned with finding techniques for the laboratory synthesis of known substances. It seems obvious that the most effective analysis and synthesis of chemical compounds will in the future be supervised by computer-based systems.

The Computer Chemist

Today computers are often much better equipped to investigate the properties of molecules than are human beings. One reason, of course, is the greater computational competence of the machine. For example, the fundamental equation of quantum theory is the wave equation first defined by Erwin Schrödinger in 1931, long before the emergence of the first electronic digital computers. Today, using a vast range of computational algorithms, the Schrödinger equation can be applied to increasingly complex chemical configurations. The relatively simple benzene molecule, for instance, contains twelve nuclei and forty-two electrons, a difficult problem even for pre-quantum mechanics. There are ways of tackling this type of problem allowing for the complexities of quantum mechanics – but it would be virtually impossible without the digital computer. Now there are many sophisticated computer programs for chemical analysis, such as ALCHEMY, ATMOL, MOLECULE and POLYATOM. In such systems there exists a computational competence that far outstrips the cleverest human chemists and mathematicians.

Studying German Verse

Computers are now developing some startling academic pretensions. For instance, they not only write poetry, but they also analyse the features of existing verse with quite remarkable insight. Steps have been taken to develop programs to investigate the sound structure of lyric verse, a difficult task using traditional methods. David Chisholm at the University of Arizona has described a rigorous computer-assisted approach to German lyric verse which identifies patterns of phonological recurrence on the basis of proximity. This effort was limited to German sonnets, and no effort was made to relate the poetic phonology to the meaning of individual poems. Now the work has extended to other poets and verse forms (including such modern poets as Rilke, Heym and Brecht). This work is far too technical to explore here – even if I understood it. Suffice it to say that, in Chisholm's words, the work 'has shown a few of the ways in which computer-assisted studies of poetic phonology can sharpen our perception of diachronic tendencies and stylistic distinctions between individual poems, verse forms, poets and periods'.

Understanding Melodic Lines

Just as computers can investigate German sonnets, so they can explore melodic lines (or 'the factors affecting the succession of tonal events in a musical composition'). One aim is to see how a composer develops his music material without violating his own sense of musical logic. Many of the problems associated with this sort of work can now be tackled by computers, though there are still a few programs equipped to tackle tasks related to music micro-analysis. One writer, David Stech from the University of Alaska, has emphasized that computers cannot be used to measure *subjectively defined* musical relationships. Some imaginative people may wonder if this is only a temporary limitation on computer competence. However, until some later date it is true that computers, engaged in musical analysis, will have to focus on the tabulations and symbol manipulations that relate to *objective* features. In short, computers may analyse music, but when will they appreciate it?

The Computer Archaeologist

If we are seeing the emergence of computer poets and computer psychiatrists, we are also seeing computers that are expert in archaeology at least in the sense that they know an immense amount about the subject. Whether computers will be able to reason in creative ways, using such knowledge, will depend upon progress in the 'rule-based knowledge-processing' systems being developed in various subject areas. Most archaeological data is not yet computerized, but many human archaeologists are aware of the need for such a facility. If computerized medical systems can diagnose diseases, it is not more difficult for computerized archaeological systems to solve archaeological problems. Already, Sylvia Gaines from Arizona State University has described computerized archaeological databases in Germany, France, Holland, Switzerland and the United Kingdom. The computer archaeologist, if not yet adult, is clearly at least in its infancy.

The Touchy Robot

Robots are developing a sense of touch, not only for work on land, but also for activities under the sea. For some years the US Naval Research Laboratory has been investigating the possibility of computer-controlled submersible vehicles that can collect rock samples, locate sunken ships, attach salvage lines to a lost object, cut holes in sunken aircraft (to remove cargo or equipment), etc. A sense of touch – often allied to sight – is useful in identifying sunken objects and in providing the data to facilitate intelligent decision-making. Robots can use segmented fingers and tactile probes to recognize natural and man-made objects. It has been suggested that a thin rod might be used for exploring deep holes and narrow cracks. Some of the simplest touch sensors are nothing more than uncomplicated micro-switches (that is, when the sensor is pressed, a circuit is made and a signal produced). An on-land robot developed by the Naval Research Laboratory has been able to locate and identify a spool of tape, using touch sensors, and then pick it up and hang it on a hook.

Computers to Brew Beer

More than one laboratory has found that computers are very efficient at controlling fermentation operations. Low-cost computers can be connected to fermenters to monitor and control the various phases of the operation. For example, the Rensselaer Polytechnic Institute (Troy, New York) has been experimenting for some time with an inexpensive microcomputer used to control fermentation operations. Sensors are used to check various parameters and feed information to the computer. Temperatures, for instance, can be monitored by thermocouples or thermistors, and sensing of pH with a glass electrode is a routine task. In fermentation processes, even a small computer can serve in the stead of many instruments. How did you manage to brew that home beer without a micro?

The Robot Work-mate

Yes-Man is a prototype robot with two arms. The device was made at Patscentre, Cambridge, for Prutec, the venture capital division of the Prudential. One idea behind the new robot is that it will be simpler than some of the existing robot systems. In the view of its designers, robots were starting to become too complicated, with manufacturers trying to make them not only manipulative but cognitive as well. It is hoped that Yes-Man, working in cooperation with human beings, will be able to take over routine laboratory tasks such as assay work, culture transfer and chemical sampling. The cognitive power of the machine is in fact a human being – an idea which must save on the artificial electronics. It is claimed that you could 'train a very unintelligent operative' to use the robot. It can be taught by taking it through the motions, or by keying in the instructions. In addition to lab work, Yes-Man could be trained to assemble keyboards, gearboxes and electric motors. In a typical use, a human being would hand Yes-Man a part, and the robot would then fit it where required. It is suggested that the robot screwdriver blades might have a retractable sheath or ultrasonic guards, for safety – and the robot arms are said to cringe when they touch human flesh!

Outprospecting the Prospectors

One of the most successful expert systems is Prospector, an intelligent computer-based facility intended to help geologists in prospecting and other tasks. In 1981 the Prospector system hit the headlines when it made a prediction that stopped more than a few geologists in their tracks. The system was given field-study data about an area in Washington State, and it concluded that there were deposits of a metal ore called molybdenum over a wide region. The human geologists disagreed and decided that the molybdenum was only present in a much more restricted area. Exploratory drilling was undertaken and the computer-based Prospector system was found to be correct. We have met computers that are variously as clever as Bertrand Russell, some Ph.D.s and international chess champions: it seems that at least one computer is cleverer than most geologists!

The Computer as Royal Accessory

Computers seem able to infiltrate any environment, even the province of the royals. President Reagan, we learn, has given the Queen of England an HP250 small business system – which doubtless she will find amazingly useful, since it includes software designed for horse-breeders, enabling them to keep mating records and to chart the pedigrees of different animals. A similar system has been installed by the Aga Khan at his French stud farm. These days even horses cannot manage to procreate without the aid of the silicon chip!

4. Military, Security and Police

'Gentlemen of the jury, you have heard the evidence . . .'

Holocaust by Computer

Alas, I cannot claim originality for this heading (try the *Guardian*, 27 January 1983). The increasing involvement of computers in military activity is one of the most disturbing aspects of modern technology. For example, computers may be programmed to respond rapidly in situations where human response times would be too slow. Intercontinental ballistic missiles – to give one example – are increasingly vulnerable to a first-strike pre-emptive attack, a circumstance that may induce military planners (still, for the most part, human beings) to deploy *launch-on-warning* systems. Satellites would be used to detect hostile missiles as soon as they were launched, infra-red radiation from the missiles would be picked up by satellite sensors and signals would be fed to computers to launch 'defensive' missiles. These missiles, launched by computer commands, would be well in flight before the incoming missiles landed. For computers to be allowed to start a nuclear holocaust, without any human decision-making, has been called 'the ultimate madness'. I will not argue with that. Perhaps, with computers developing their *own* survival strategies, we will be forced to rely on *their* good sense in the face of human folly.

The War-making Computer I

One of the most legitimate fears about nuclear war is the possibility of a catastrophic accident. Sometimes computers don't do much to allay our fears. One famous false alarm occurred on 3 June 1980: a faulty computer indicated that a missile attack was about to be launched against the United States. It is said that the entire North American defence command was alerted. In fact much anxiety has been expressed about the reliability of the computer-based Worldwide Military Command and Control System (known as Wimex) run by the Americans. In one estimate in the early 1980s it was stated that there were ten false alerts for every one the Press is told of: the system was said to fail not less than once every thirty-five minutes! Among a catalogue of potentially disastrous blunders, the system has mistaken a rolling bank of fog and a flock of geese for Soviet missile attacks. It has been said that US military leaders would not believe Wimex if, for once, it got it right! As far back as 1976, General Alexander Haig was quoted as saying that Wimex 'is generally considered to be inefficient and approaching obsolescence'. And the three dozen or so Wimex computers operate in such a complex system that it is difficult to see how they could ever be rendered sufficiently reliable to prevent the launch, through system faults, of World War III. Arthur C. Clarke has observed that future wars will start in the circuits of computers rather than in the minds of men.

The War-making Computer II

If the idea of generals running wars is horrific enough, the idea of computers being given the job must be more so. Yet today various companies, mainly in the US, are investigating how computers could do this. For example, Ed Taylor, of TRW Defense Systems in California, runs a government-funded research effort aiming to develop a computer that can make the right tactical decisions as consistently as the best generals. (Taylor has observed: 'The main problem with fighting a modern war is that you have good generals and dumb generals.') Part of the research involves observing what 'good' generals do in war games that 'bad' generals do not do; then the expertise (the 'judgemental ability') can be fed into a computer. It is thought that the first automated system should be up and running by 1990 – so you've got until then to write your will. Similar research is focusing on how computers can store medical expertise to diagnose human illness, so there is a nice balance in these various pieces of research: one computer explodes the nuclear bombs while another is wheeled on to diagnose the extent of radiation sickness in the handful of survivors.

Where to Bomb Next

Computers are now making judgements, not only about how sick people should be treated or what materials are best suited to a particular type of aircraft wing, but about how to conduct the minutiae of military conflict. There is already evidence of this. Many observers have expressed concern about how computers were allowed a judgemental role in the Vietnam war (in due course we may hear about the same sort of thing in connection with the Falklands conflict). We can quote the computer scientist, Joseph Weizenbaum: 'During the Vietnam war, computers operated by officers who had not the slightest idea of what went on inside their machines effectively chose which hamlets were to be bombed.' The Vietnamese, we may remark, had no computers – and they were the winners.

Computer Specifies Casualties

The UK government, like other governments, sometimes engages in efforts to estimate the number of likely casualties in the event of nuclear war. Some people (for instance, Duncan Campbell in *War Plan UK*) have suggested that the government sometimes misrepresents the danger to make nuclear war seem less horrific than it would certainly be. Campbell has quoted a computer analysis which shows that in one scenario of nuclear war there would be 29 million corpses in the United Kingdom (this is the so-called 'Square Leg' scenario). However, by using unrealistic 'protective factors' the Home Office managed to reduce the likely number of deaths to only (!) three million. This is an interesting point. Program your computer carefully and it will give you the figures you want, even if these relate to dead bodies. At the same time, computer-generated data carries a bogus authority, a useful device for unscrupulous politicians.

The Radiation Robot

A plastic robot with artificial organs is being used at the Brookhaven National Laboratory in the United States for monitoring radiation doses. The robot is said to have comparable radiation absorption properties to those of a human being. I doubt, however, that after a few weeks it loses its hair and bleeds from bodily orifices.

The War-gaming Computer

Computers are proving useful in waging imaginary wars as well as real ones. The use of computers in fanciful war games has the advantage that only imaginary people get killed – but the disadvantage that game practitioners tend to believe that wars, even nuclear ones, are winnable. (This is not to mention technical criticisms of war-gaming theory.) Desmond Ball has described some of the statistics that go into American war-game exercises. In American strategic target planning, there are more than 40,000 potential Soviet targets. These include the Soviet nuclear forces (2,000 targets), about 20,000 other military targets, the Soviet military and political leadership (about 3,000 targets), and about 15,000 economic and industrial targets. In one estimate, the US currently has about 10,000 operational strategic nuclear warheads. In an official computer study, described by Ball, it is assumed that the American strategic weapons are launched before any Soviet weapons explode in the US. The computer suggests that about 8,700 targets would be destroyed in the Soviet Union (2,000 involving nuclear forces, 1,600 other military targets, 740 leadership targets, and 4,400 economic and industrial targets). This study seemingly imagines a first strike by America, something that we do not see much discussion about in the West.

The Computer Gunners

We see that computers are likely to be running wars before long. At a more modest level, computers are also happy controlling the guns on tanks. In 1983 the Royal Ordnance Factory at Leeds delivered the first Challenger tank, complete with computerized gun, to the British Army. Computer control is required so that the tank can shoot accurately at moving targets, even when the vehicle itself is being driven hard across country. Sensors are used to measure wind speed, direction, air temperature and other factors that might affect the flight of the shell. The human gunner sights an enemy tank (doubtless a Soviet one) and employs a laser to measure the range, whereupon the appropriate information is fed to the computer. Motors are then automatically instructed to slew the turret and raise the gun barrel to the appropriate position. In such a way, the gun can operate accurately over two thousand metres. Challenger is to be fitted with thermal imagers so that targets can be seen at night. It may be, of course, that a Challenger tank will be destroyed first by a computerized gun operated by a Soviet gunner. It is one of the curious paradoxes of war that the God-fearing do not have a monopoly of murderous weaponry.

Training Those Tank Drivers

The Rundle Instruments Division of Purdy Machinery is to supply a number of optical probe devices for the Singer simulator system for training tank drivers. We are used to hearing about pilots being trained on simulators, but there is less publicity for the training of tank gunners and tank drivers. The specially designed probes feed a servo-controlled closed-circuit television system to relay information from the simulated terrain (a defined scale model is provided of suitable territory) to the trainee driver. It is possible to use the system, with only minor adjustments, for other fighting vehicles, and British aerospace companies are said to be interested in the possibilities. The optical probe system provides good colour and a high level of realism to achieve an effective simulation. But how realistic are such simulations when actual war conditions are envisaged? Are there competing tanks (with, doubtless, their own computer-based facilities)? Is there general smoke, evident carnage and a nuclear explosion or two? Simulation for war purposes can only be assessed after the war has taken place. Many of us may feel that this would be an unwelcome experiment.

The Robot Munitions-maker

Computers are becoming increasingly involved in war-planning and war-making – and they are assisted by their brother (and sister?) robots in the manufacture of shells and other projectiles. Some arsenals are now using robots as projectile depalletizing systems. Empty projectiles arrive at the arsenals after being forged and machined. They arrive on wooden pallets and are then transported to an area for loading into tank cars. The robot system is required to remove and dispose of banding, protective plastic grommets and the pallet tops. Four 4000A Unimate robots are used to handle the projectiles. One robot engages a lift lug and unscrews it, and a second robot in one of the two-robot teams picks up the projectile by engaging the internal threads in the nose and transferring the part to a tank car. The robots have appropriate hands for the task: one includes a contoured cup and lift pin, the other comprises an internal expanding mandrel for transporting the projectile. Arsenals have the problem that they are under most pressure at times of national crisis. Robots capable of flexible operation help to answer this problem, and they also free men from the hazardous environment of munitions manufacture.

The Robot Missile-maker

Robots, working in friendly cooperation with machine tools, are now making missile fins. For example, in one application, two Unimate robots are being used to process missile fins through no less than eight separate machining stages. A (human) machinist puts the fins into a drilling machine, after which the robots take over. One takes the parts from the drilling machine and feeds them through three successive borematic processes – rough-machining, semi-finishing and finishing. A robot with a ten-foot reach is used to feed the finished parts through the other stages of manufacture: for example, complex slots are then cut into the various surfaces of the fin hub. Again, the robots have specially designed hands for the tasks in question: two toggle-type hands are employed and, interestingly enough, the fingers carry rubber pads to avoid marking the parts. Do they not even leave fingerprints (see 'The Computerized Andy Warhol, p. 168)?

The Computerized Fighter

Just as computers are making torpedoes and missiles more effective, so they are helping to enhance the killing power of aircraft. Marconi Avionics has developed computer-controlled radar for the interceptor version of the Tornado multi-role combat aircraft. A central programmable computer has been designed into the radar and there are distributed processing facilities throughout the equipment. A main computer has up to 32,000 words of store capacity, and in addition there are 'well over a dozen' Motorola microprocessors. The radar uses fast Fourier transform analysis to track targets through heavy unwanted reflections (clutter). This computerized radar is supposed to have the ability to track more than two dozen targets simultaneously, and the computer can be doing various other things at the same time. For example, it can continue to search for new targets while updating the data on those which have already been found. Tornado is intended to carry radar-directed guided missiles, called Sky Flash, and the Sidewinder short-range missiles, which are also amenable to radar control. Presumably the Russian Backfire supersonic bombers – which the Tornadoes would be expected to attack – also have a few computer tricks up their sleeves!

The Computerized Torpedo

The British Royal Navy and Royal Air Force now has a computerized torpedo, called Sting Ray, which is supposed to be effective against any Soviet submarines. Sting Ray, developed by Marconi Space and Defence Systems, has cost nearly £1,000 million to develop and is intended to replace the American-designed Mk 44 and Mk 46 torpedoes. It can be launched from surface warships, from helicopters such as the Lynx and Sea King, and from Nimrod anti-submarine aircraft. Sting Ray is reckoned to be the first guided weapon in the world to use a programmable digital computer. The system analyses sounds picked up by the acoustic sensors and compares them with stored information. This allows the computer to distinguish between submarines and other underwater objects, and also between enemy and friendly vessels! The computer is supposed to be too bright to be confused by decoys and other counter-measures. The on-board computer has also been designed to have unusually low power requirements – so Sting Ray's batteries last longer. Marconi have commented that this scale of investment would be hard to justify in commercial terms. But, after all, what government worries about military spending?

Computers as Missile Pilots

Whatever the political debates about Cruise missiles, there can be little doubt that they are ingenious devices. The early Boeing Air-Launched cruise Missile (ALCM), for instance, is a manoeuvrable unmanned, self-guided weapon capable of reading the terrain over which it flies. It compares radar readings with maps stored in its computer memory, guiding itself through the enemy's defence systems to a predetermined target. Cruise is small and flies at low altitude (at about thirty metres over flat country). It is supposed to be able to carry a 200-kiloton warhead (ten times as powerful as the Hiroshima bomb) to within thirty metres of a target up to 3,600 kilometres away. (At the time of writing, Britain has just become host to the amiable cruise systems; and there are reports that the Soviet Union is designing similar weapons of its own.)

Exocet and Friends

The Exocet radar-homing missile first gained extensive publicity in the West when it sank the British destroyer, H.M.S. *Sheffield* on 4 May 1982. It has been pointed out that the *Sheffield* was a highly rated ship, built about ten years ago at a cost of approximately £28 million. Exocet, by contrast, cost well under one million pounds. Exocet is now seen as one of a growing family of 'smart' anti-ship missiles. Other such missiles are the Gabriel Mk III (Israel), the Harpoon RGM-84A (US), the Tomahawk BGM-109 (US), the Styx SS-N-2C (USSR) and the Kitchen AS-4 (USSR). Such missiles store target data in their memories, just as the cruise missile does, and process changing trajectory information to home in on a target. The so-called 'smart missiles' are commonplace in the arsenals of the world. Even Libya, for example, is now reported to have no less than thirteen kinds of smart missiles in its arsenal. Today large traditional ships are immensely vulnerable (*Sheffield* was supposed to have many modern and effective defensive systems). With computer-guided missiles, possibly carrying nuclear warheads, the next big war will be short. Retired Admiral Rickover testified in 1982 that a modern aircraft carrier would last about two days in a major war. We may also reckon that the main belligerents would have few towns or cities left standing by then.

The Odex 1 Functionoid – Sentry, Spaceman, Cop . . .

The robot is one of the most exciting developments in modern technology. In this book you will come across a few examples of the species – or are there already many different species? Here we can briefly introduce Odex 1, a worthy friend to Cubot, LUIGI *et al.*, who perform ably in these pages. Odex 1 is about two metres tall and weighs 370 pounds (168 kg). The fellow can lift several times its own weight, and by means of its six legs it can move steadily on rough terrain. The California company, Odetics, has produced Odex 1 as a planned family of *functionoids* – yet another buzz-word for robot buffs. Odex 1 runs off a 24-volt aircraft battery and can climb stairs, changing its posture and gait as necessary. But what use is it? The list of possible applications is endless; the makers reckon that functionoids could be used for mine clearing, sentry duty, space exploration, fire-fighting, surveillance, law enforcement, forestry work and for activities in nuclear power stations. So, if you come across a tin-can insect directing the traffic, you know where it came from . . .

The Robot Soldier

We see, in the 1980s, that computers are getting round to the idea of running our wars – but the idea of an automated soldier has been around for a long time. As far back as 1939, a robot soldier was shown at the New York Exhibition. This contraption was about 2.75 metres tall, weighed half a ton, and was radio-controlled. Its two legs, each with a caterpillar track, moved under the power of an 18-horsepower motor. The robot's arms carried clubs, and the device was said to be able to exude asphyxiating gases. We have not seen much of him since, certainly not in any war or civil control situation – presumably because he would make such an easy target!

The Wheelbarrow Bomb-detector

In Northern Ireland, the British Army uses a robot bomb-detector. This device, called 'wheelbarrow', consists of a television camera mounted on a flexible arm surmounting a tank-like base. A video display, well out of the danger zone, shows what the robot can see. Under remote control, the vehicle trundles to a suspect area and moves around, looking for bombs. 'Wheelbarrow' also contains a number of devices for defusing bombs. It is also reported (*Computer Decisions*, February 1977) that the system is in use by the Argentine police to detonate explosive devices (what happens to 'wheelbarrow' in these circumstances?). This system was sold to the Argentine military (and to the British Army?) by E-Systems, a Texas supplier of military and police electronics. (E-Systems purchased Air Asia in 1975 from the Air America Company, owned and operated by the CIA.)

The Secretive Computer

Computers often contribute to a 'Big-Brother' image of modern society. Take the case of GCHQ (the intelligence system and headquarters at Cheltenham) and its links with the US National Security Agency (NSA). Following the secret UK/USA treaty (1947), GCHQ was linked with NSA, and the two organizations have cooperated ever since. An NSA officer has declared: 'There are three satellites over the Atlantic, each capable of transmitting on about 20,000 circuits. There are eight transatlantic cables with about 5,000 circuits. *We monitor them all*' (my italics). The computers of NSA – which can home in on a signal if they detect a keyword – cover eleven acres. The computers can search for keywords at the rate of four million characters a second. This means that the computers could read and index a newspaper before you could pronounce its name. And GCHQ and NSA have 'watch lists' of groups and individuals whose communications are automatically intercepted. These have included civil rights groups, newspapers, politicians, trade missions, etc.

The Security Computer

The idea of computer-based security has a significant history, but it was the emergence of the microprocessor that made it possible to build automated security into a wide range of commercial systems. For example, Norgrange Ltd, retained by Thor Security, has developed systems based on the Apple II microcomputer. Peter Took (of Norgrange) has observed: 'The biggest danger to a security system – no matter how sophisticated – is false alarms. If the local police force is used to investigate these alerts, they might become sceptical when future alarms are given or even refuse to act. If the site uses its own reaction force, the same problems apply.' Microcomputers bring reliability to security measures. Moreover, speed of response is often vital where there is a breach of security. A computer can be programmed to take over from a security officer if he is reacting too slowly. And the computer is clever enough to detect which are those troublesome false alarms!

The Repressive Computer

Computers, like much machinery, can lend themselves to political repression. Not very long ago, there was agitation about the uses to which ICL computer systems were being put in South Africa. In fact they were making it easier for the authorities to run an authoritarian and undemocratic political system. And in South America, computers supplied by the United States are being used to aid regimes that rely on torture and other appalling methods of repression. According to the reputable trade journal *Computer Decisions* (February 1977), US firms were selling sophisticated computer systems to Chile, Uruguay, Argentina and Brazil to help the authorities to locate political suspects for interrogation, torture and subsequent elimination. This prompted the authors of the journal article to ask 'Would You Sell Computers to Hitler?'

Big Brother and Telephones

Computerization of telephone exchanges may come to have totalitarian consequences. For example, one consequence may be that telephone conversations will be much more easily tapped – by the authorities or by anyone else. Yet again, the computer may come to embody a repressive function. More than one observer has suggested that human freedoms are best protected by bureaucratic inefficiencies. Computers, alas, tend to make things less inefficient – when, that is, the bureaucracies favour that sort of development.

Silicon-chip Security

Car thieves have often proved themselves to be ingenious fellows, but will they master the silicon chip? We all know that silicon chips are abundant in modern cars – if we are to believe what the chips are telling us. But one of the first uses of chip technology in automobiles was to provide enhanced security. One chip-based system prevents the car from starting until a 'personal pre-programmed four-digit code' is keyed in on a special keyboard control unit. How are the thieves to overcome this one? Doubtless the putative villains are working on it.

Computerized Hit-and-run Detection

Computers are helping the police in various ways (if they are also helping criminals, which seems highly unlikely, we hear less about it). One recently introduced device is a colour-identifying minicomputer being used by the Scientific Investigation Research Laboratory of the Tokyo Police Bureau. From fragments of paint left at sites of automobile accidents, the system is supposed to be able to identify criminals and hit-and-run drivers by pinpointing vehicle type and year model within five minutes. No less than 10,000 paints are currently stored in the computer memory.

Breath Test by Computer

Once the computer has brewed your beer for you (see p. 42), it can help the police to test your breath. Blowing into balloons is not always considered reliable enough for court evidence, and the process usually has to be followed by blood or urine tests, which involve a doctor who may feel he has better things to do. Now the UK Home Office is considering introducing computerized breath-analysis machines. Yes, you still have to blow, but the result is considered to be accurate enough to be used as evidence. The legal limit − 80 milligrams of alcohol to 100 millilitres of blood − becomes expressed, under the new system, as 35 micrograms to 100 millilitres of air. We are all pleased to know that.

The Computer as Victim

Some people worry that computers will one day get the upper hand, a theme rehearsed *ad nauseam* in science fiction. Today, in the 1980s, we can still 'pull out the plug' if the machine gets too stroppy, so cutting off its food supply. And on occasions we resort to more drastic measures. Thus, in August 1978, a depressed postal inspector rushed into the computer room of Montpellier's main post office in Southern France, and opened fire on the computer. It was injured by five bullets − whether fatally, I do not know − while the sole human employee present hid under a table. In a more recent case (reported in *Human Factors and Information Technology*, National Electronics Council, 1983), an American police officer fired two bullets into a computer terminal. The interactive system had responded once too often with 'I do not understand'.

5. The Creative Computer

'It's decided to go solo . . .'

The Computer Poets

Computer poetry has been influenced by a discovery made by Louis Milic, an English professor at Cleveland State University, working with computer-generated prose. Some computer-produced sentences (for instance, 'A shirt thought with a dog'), albeit seemingly nonsensical, made some people think about poetry. Milic asked: 'Why would a sentence generated by a computer be mistaken for poetry?' The following two poetic excerpts have been compared:

> Because the pleasure-bird whistles
> after the hot wires,
> Shall the blind horse swing sweeter?

> What does she put four whistles
> beside the heated rugs for?

The first extract is by Dylan Thomas; the second was written by a computer. Milic in fact took some of Thomas's poems and let a computer rearrange them, and his students could not always tell which poems were genuine and which had been doctored. Later a Milic program, Erato, was written to scramble words from famous poems, an operation that has suggested various poetic insights. Today, computers can write poetry. First they have to be taught how – but then so do human poets.

Computerized Haiku

Computers have been programmed to write various types of poetry. They have, for instance, written Japanese haiku, often with unexpected results. A haiku is a three-line poem of seventeen syllables, with the lines containing respectively five, seven and five syllables. The subject matter of a haiku is not restricted but there should be a reference to the season of the year. Here is a typical computer-generated haiku:

> All green in the leaves,
> I smell dark pools in the trees.
> Crash! The moon has fled.

In programming a computer to write poetry, it is necessary to set up a 'frame', to create a thesaurus, and to devise systems which can be employed to operate on the thesaurus (a sonnet requires a more complex frame than does a haiku). Computers so programmed often achieve results that go far beyond the programmer's expectations.

The Computer Love-poet

Computers can not only write poetry, they can write love-poetry. Ron Clark, for instance, taught a Radio Shack TRS-80 Color Computer how to write sentences and how to create verse. He also gave the computer a vocabulary, after which the computer was able to create 'some very thought-provoking love poems'. Sixty-six of the poems are published in *My Buttons Are Blue* (ARCsoft, 1982), each of the poems being, according to

Clark, 'the result of contemplation and insightful formation by the solid-state digital circuits . . .'. Here is a portion from one of the poems:

> Long bald boys
> Humanize toughly around the bend,
> Where crunchy glowing friends
> Turn sweetly to the wind.
>
> Light carved cats
> Run wetly toward our lives,
> Where hard short wives
> Humanize tenderly in the night.

Perhaps our traditional human poets had better look to their laurels – or perhaps not.

A Computer Fable-writer

A famous program written by Jim Meehan in 1976, called Tale-Spin, is able to create stories akin to Aesop's fables. Engaging characters are given motives – hunger, thirst, sleepiness, sex (referred to by Tale-Spin as 'fooling around'), etc. – whereupon the plot is allowed to unfold. A typical Tale-Spin fable runs as follows:

> Once upon a time George Ant lived near a patch of ground. There was a nest in an ash tree. Wilma Bird lived in the nest. There was some water in a river . . . One day Wilma was very thirsty . . . Wilma flew from her nest across a meadow through a valley to the river. Wilma drank the water. Wilma wasn't thirsty any more.

The full story, of which this is a brief sample, is seen to be akin to traditional folk-tales.

The Computer Novelist

Yes, 'novelist' *is* a rather extravagant description of computers as story-tellers. Computer efforts in this area are rudimentary, to say the least. At the same time, they are not without significance. Sheldon Klein, for instance, at the University of Wisconsin, collaborated with his students to produce a program (the Novel Writer Simulation Program) that could write 2,100-word mystery stories in nineteen seconds each. In fact, *Murder Mystery 1* was written by a Univac 1108 computer, and was first presented at the International Conference on Computers in the Humanities (Minneapolis, July 1973). To whet your appetite, here is the start of the story: 'Wonderful smart Lady Buxley was rich. Ugly oversexed Lady Buxley was single. John was Lady Buxley's nephew. Impoverished irritable John was evil . . .' Perhaps human novelists don't need to worry about competition from machines just yet! In mid-1984, Warner Books published *The Policeman's Beard is Half Constructed*, the first book written by a computer – by, in fact, the Racter story-writing program. Racter himself has observed: 'This book is about delight and satisfaction and joy . . .'

The Science-fiction Writer

Gulliver's word-machine (p. 11) anticipated one of the approaches to poem-writing and story-writing by computer. All you do is build up a store of words, concepts, phrases, expressions, etc., then provide a frame or structure, and finally let the computer randomly select from the store to fill in the parts of the structure. Hey presto! An 'original' artistic creation is the result. A flow chart has been produced to enable a computer to write a science-fiction story (it first appeared in Sam Lundwall's *Science Fiction: An Illustrated History* and is reproduced in Adrian Berry's *The Super-Intelligent Machine*). The chart has a set of stages through which you (or the computer) proceed sequentially. At each stage, one of several options is chosen; with different story features selected on each run-through, many different – though equally banal – tales can be generated. This may hardly seem an effective way of writing stories (in science fiction or anything else). But who can say that the *actual* 'creative task' undertaken by human beings trying to write an original tale proceeds in a radically different way to this? All we do is manipulate, and choose from, our store of facts, concepts and imaginings. The science-fiction flow chart allows for both sad and happy endings: temperament or randomized computer activity decides which type of ending is selected.

Composing the Illiac Suite

Computers have been skilled musical composers for some time. Some systems can write original melodies (for example, following the style of Mozart); others can write harmonies for existing tunes. One of the most significant developments in the area of composition was that associated with Hiller and Isaacson in 1955 and 1956. Working at the University of Illinois, they accumulated enough output to assemble the *Illiac Suite for String Quartet*, a composition which comprised four 'Experiments'. Experiment I produced melodies and four-part harmony; Experiment II elaborated the composition by employing fourteen stylistic rules, typical of such sixteenth-century composers as Palestrina; Experiment III generated variety of rhythm and other musical dynamics combined with occasional dissonance, and produced music of a twentieth-century style; and Experiment IV composed without reference to any particular historical style, using a table of probabilities to set the intervals between notes. Broadly conceived, the Illiac music exploited a few elementary symbols, chosen at random, with composition rules used to link them in acceptable arrangements. A corollary to this work is the mathematical analysis of the works of the great composers: computers will soon not only be able to synthesize any musical sound but also compose music in the style of any historical composer.

Melody by Computer

It is relatively easy for a computer to write a melody, but it is much harder for a computer to generate a truly interesting melody, a tune with some musical significance. Various research programmes have emerged as relevant to the computer generation of music. For example, IBM work on the mathematics of shapes has been shown to relate to the shape of melody. It has become clear that too much order (or too little) is undesirable in effective musical composition. What is required is a clear direction plus an element of chance. Even topics such as the flood levels of the River Nile and the shapes of coastlines have been seen to bear on the theory of useful musical composition: underlying patterns can hold together the general structure of the composition. Effective melodies have been composed by the Fractal program (the word 'fractal' was coined to describe events that have a significant underlying unity). Another musical-composition program derived from a study of Schoenberg's early atonal melodies – appropriately enough, this program has been dubbed 'Schoenberg'.

Learning to Harmonize

Computers can write melodies and also harmonies for existing ones. For instance, a system has been developed at Nottingham University which, when given the line of a musical melody, will produce a chord sequence to accompany the melody. The system currently uses traditional British folk-tunes, mainly derived from social dances, but also from songs and ceremonial dances. Parameters are included to allow the characteristics of the accompaniment to be easily varied. It is conceded that the harmonies generated 'are not perfect', but none the less they have produced a number of 'interesting possibilities'. The system can, for instance, reliably 'produce the expected boring harmonies in simple situations'. We are not surprised to learn that there is 'much scope for further development and research'. Perhaps most interesting are some of the bibliographic entries in the paper by E. Foxley (in *IUCC Bulletin*, Vol. 3, 1981): these include *One Thousand Fiddle Tunes*, *Collections of Merry Melodies*, and *Ceol Rince na h'Eirann* in Gaelic.

The Mozart Computer

There is a way of composing instant Mozart by means of a little known opus called the *Dice Waltz*. This work has been seen as, in effect, an automatic generator of minuets. Mozart began by assembling 176 musical bars of two types, suitable for the two parts that would comprise each of the generated minuets. Then the two groups of bars were arranged into tables, and the bars to be chosen were selected simply by throwing a pair of dice. It has been remarked that this Mozartian effort almost suggests that the great composer had computers in mind. Today a computer program has been written to allow the 'dice' to be thrown on a video display. The dice tumble across the screen, displaying the desired numbers on their top faces. After sixteen throws a table is constructed. The resulting music generated by the dice sequence can be printed on manuscript displayed on the screen, or hard copy can be produced if a printer is available. After supplying prompts for volume and tempo, the music can be played through in three-part harmony. The idea behind the *Dice Waltz* suggests that Mozart would have been highly sympathetic to this means of generating minuets.

The Computerized Music Show

Computers are affecting the arts in many ways. One recent example is a computerized music show, the 'Contemporary Music Network', that cruised round the UK in early 1983. This effort, supported by the Arts Council, was supervised by Tim Souster who wrote the music for *Hitchhiker's Guide to the Galaxy*. A new piece he wrote for the tour is mysteriously entitled, *The Transistor Radio of St Narcissus*, the finale of which has been described as 'splendidly purple, with a marching pop-flavoured bass surmounted by the triumphant solo in far-flung multiplication'. Think what we would have missed without such computer-stimulated efforts!

Play it Again, Computer!

Dr Robert Moog – perhaps more than any other person responsible for the development of the music synthesizer – has declared: 'The time is fast approaching when no self-respecting rock band will be without its own computer. The bass player, the drummer, the soundman and the lighting engineer will all have interfaces to it. Computers are the most versatile tools that musicians have ever had to work with.' Paradoxically, Moog declares that electronic music is a category of music, and still reckons that the computer is only a tool (but see pp. 62–3 on musical composition). It has been suggested that the fifth-generation of musical instruments is characterized by the use of computers. A synthesizer can store any actual sound, and reproduce it at the touch of a key. Stored sounds can be reproduced polyphonically (to produce chords). Even Herbert von Karajan has relied upon a synthesizer – computer-based, of course – to reproduce the ringing of bells in a performance of *Parsifal*.

The Music Unit Generator

Max V. Mathews of Bell Laboratories in New Jersey has made prodigious contributions to computer-generated music. His development of unit generators has been represented as a great conceptual advance. These electronic signal generating devices may be regarded as individual instruments that the composer can use as sonic building-blocks. Electronic control makes it possible to generate sounds in real time: thus, by pushing a button, the composer can create sounds of amazing complexity. Mathews has at times seemed ambivalent about the quality of some of his musical compositions: he has even described some of his pieces as 'musically nauseating', a judgement with which certain traditional musical purists may agree. It has been suggested that his efforts at musical composition are overshadowed by his achievements as instrument builder and musical analyst. Mathews is also famous for his Music IV and Music V programs which enable musicians to work with the computer without being daunted by technical concerns.

The Compu-Music Computer

There are now many products available that exploit computer power in the reproduction and composition of music. Using the Roland Compu-Music system, manufactured by the Roland Corporation (California), it is possible for a computer to synthesize any kind of music. The system can churn out, according to the advertising blurb, '. . . a waltz, a blues song, a rhapsody, and a whole lotta rock n roll'. The makers suggest that the system can be used by anyone – from the computer user with a programming background to the programmer 'with a song in his heart'. It is reckoned that such a device has done for music what the word processor has done for words. Compu-Music software enables the home computer to write, program, change and store musical works of up to eight voices, if necessary in conjunction with a seven-voice electronic drummer. The hardware (CMU-800) is an effective music synthesizer designed to play these musical parts. Now if all this sounds like a commercial, it's not surprising. It is culled from an advertisement. But the scope of the system deserves mention. All this is yet another sign that musicians and composers will one day be largely supplanted by fancy silicon chips.

The Computer Organist

Microcomputers can now learn to operate pipe organs – perhaps not to take over from the human player, but to ease his task considerably. Moreover, use of a micro can be much less expensive than all that console wiring. A microcomputer in a pipe organ is typically required to keep watch on 500 switches and to control 6,000 relays, one for each pipe. It cannot afford to miss a switch closure or release, and must always operate the correct pipes (sometimes working dozens simultaneously) within one twentieth of a second. You may wonder if a simple microcomputer can cope with all this. Seemingly it can. And there are many reasons for wanting it to try. We have mentioned cost and ease of use. There are also a variety of gimmicks that may amuse some folk. For example, a micro-controlled organ could be induced automatically to play 'Jesu, Joy of Man's Desiring' – or anything else – at full volume, whenever a visitor presses the door button. And the traditional appearance of the organ could stay the same. It could appear nicely seasoned by age, though computerized to the hilt.

Music-making Again

One consequence of the proliferation of microcomputers is that many small systems are now engaged in making music. Pretty well every micro on the market has some kind of sound generator. The Apple II and Apple III, for instance, have built-in speakers, and the cassette port of the TRS-80 can be used to make music. But perhaps the Atari 400 and 800 are the most impressive systems for this sort of purpose. Each Atari carries a four-voice synthesizer, with each voice able to sound a single note at various volumes and with various tonal qualities. Since four separate notes can be sounded at one time, it is possible to play musical chords. Different programs can be written to enable this to be accomplished in various different ways. Of one such program, an author writes: 'It won't win you a Grammy Award, but with this chord organ program you'll begin to appreciate the music capability of the Atari.'

A Program to Write Operas

As well as devising programs to write stories (see 'The Computer Novelist', pp. 60–1), Sheldon Klein and his students at the University of Wisconsin have invented a program to write operas. The opera-writer, like the story-writing programs, has two parts. A simulator is used to generate the plot in a special symbolic language devised by the group, and then translators are employed to turn the symbolic plot into words, music, and moving pictures of the action. Two computers are used for opera-generation: an Apple micro produces the music, and a Terak computer is used to produce the other required functions. The name of the simulation language, engagingly enough, is pronounced 'bar-bar'. The resulting opera is based on Edwin Abbott's nineteenth-century fantasy *Flatland*. Klein has remarked: 'I'm not keen on showing it because, to be perfectly frank, the music is superb but the action is quite dull.' And he has noted that the computer-generated opera could be five hours long, like a real opera, 'but at the end there would be nobody watching'.

Painting by Digits

Computers are not content just to do sums: it has been obvious for some time that they are keen to have a crack at musical composition and graphic art. One computer artist is David Em, the Artist-in-Residence at the Jet Propulsion Laboratory in Pasadena. A computer is helping him to produce 'paintings' of startling originality, which has stimulated weighty thought about the creative capacity of computers. David Em uses a PDP-11/55 computer to generate abstract pictures of a dreamlike, or even nightmarish quality. He can select from 256 colours and a range of electronic 'brushes' to vary the effect. Photographic prints and lithographs have been produced from the displays. Em has declared that the system 'leads me to trains of thought that would never have occurred to me without the computer'. Furthermore, he feels he is working with an 'infinite' machine: 'The medium is only at the Neanderthal stage.' One journalistic observer has remarked that maybe the days of the artist in the garret are numbered!

6. Computers in Transport

Honeysett

'*It's not very encouraging I'm afraid Mr Nisbett.
I fed your symptoms into the computer and it died.*'

The Imaginary Walking Robot

We see that some robots are walking in the real world, using their two or
more legs (and there is also a one-legged hopping robot). What is also
remarkable is that robots can be simulated (imagined) by computer systems
in order to test their possible responses in (imaginary) terrain. For example, a
typical simulation program has facilities for representing both the vehicle and
the terrain, to investigate how one interacts with the other. In one system of
this sort, the program is run on a DEC-10 computer and use is made of an
AG-60 plasma panel display as an output device. A simplified depiction of the
vehicle is shown from the top, with, in this case, its 'reachable areas'
corresponding to those of a defined hexapod system. In this fascinating
mobile display, only the *supporting* legs are shown at any one time, since the
positions of any legs in the air are irrelevant to vehicle stability. Many

different types of terrain can be studied in this 'imaginary' way, with different types of robot gait scrutinized for efficient operation.

The Motor-cycle Computer

We all know that cars are finding themselves equipped with computers, designed variously to economize on fuel, plot routes or act as a surrogate back-seat driver. But we are less used to hearing mention of computers infiltrating motorbikes. Today the Honda CX 500 Turbo motorcycle has a computer to ensure that each cylinder receives the right amount of fuel. Moreover, the device can also check on atmospheric pressure, temperature and how far you have opened the throttle. A variety of sensors are also linked to the computer to indicate a variety of possible faults. Why should anything ever go wrong?

The Computer Bus-controller

For some years microcomputers have been used to control fleets of buses. In 1979 the UK company IAL sold a microchip system to control the 250-bus fleet of the San Mateo County Transit Authority, just south of San Francisco. Each driver carries a microcomputer beside him, linked to a two-way radio. The central dispatcher is thus enabled to know the departure and arrival times and the number of passengers on any vehicle. The micros help to avoid route congestion and also provide a wide range of management information. Furthermore, the microcomputers use sensors on the buses to monitor oil levels, brake fluid, and engine temperature. If a critical value is reached for any of the monitored parameters the dispatcher is automatically alerted. A hidden emergency button also allows the driver to alert headquarters in the event of a robbery: headquarters can identify the relevant bus and listen in, whereupon, we assume, they can take appropriate action.

The Robot Truck

Warwick University, with Lansing Bagnall, is developing an automatic free-roving industrial truck. This may be the forerunner of a family of mobile robotic devices. Trucks *can* be guided by underfloor guide-wires, but such a method is self-evidently a 'fixed' guidance system, allowing for no flexibility of movement. The alternative is to provide a vehicle with a navigation system, sensory devices, an on-board controller, a communications facility and other systems. The Warwick University free-roving truck uses sonar sensing devices, which in turn are based on the low-cost range-finding system found in cameras. The truck is thereby able to receive advance warning of an obstacle, and to calculate what evasive action should be taken. The free-ranging truck, in fact, aims to follow a route to a defined destination. It carries an on-board map for this purpose, the map including 'marker buoys' which the control system checks as the journey proceeds. If the truck is unable to evade an obstacle, it avoids collision by stopping, at the same time sending out a message requesting assistance. When the machine is confident (when there are few evident obstacles), it speeds along, but in a hazardous environment it moves with caution!

The Soviet Robot

Soviet robot research gets little exposure in the West, though we may expect the Soviet philosophy, wedded to science as it purports to be, to show an interest in such matters. At the twenty-sixth Congress of the Communist Party of the Soviet Union, Leonid Brezhnev declared that the USSR would have 50,000 industrial robots by 1985 ('Russia will build 40,000 robots during the current five-year plan'). Stepping excavators have been used to clear forests in Siberia, and the Soviet writer Artobolevsky has described a four-legged vehicle called a 'mechanized horse' which weighs 1.5 tonnes, is 3 metres long, and is powered by a 90-horsepower automobile engine. He also refers to a strange sort of train used for military transport: it has carriages on legs which can either push or pull. It can travel through mud, sand and gravel, and even pass between trees that are as little as fifty-one inches apart. Do such things exist? It seems highly unlikely.

The Imaginary Driver

Computers can now imagine what it is to be like a car driver. The UK Transport and Road Research Laboratory has developed programs to simulate driver behaviour. The computer driver can be induced to behave much as a human being would at varying speeds and different weather conditions. Scientists have concluded that most drivers can be categorized into eight fundamental types, depending upon about six quantifiable parameters (such as determination and anticipation). This sort of behavioural data can be fed into a computer and a simulated test-run plotted. The results have closely accorded with results obtained from the same drives in real life. Such work is seen as relevant to car design, energy consumption and other factors. It is ironic that a computer driver *of this sort* may be required to drive 'badly', to respond much as would a human being in particular circumstances. A *real* automated driver, computer-based and capable of rapid response, is likely to be much more competent than the average human being.

Isn't One Back-seat Driver Enough?

No self-respecting new car design can fail to include a computer or two – though some of the applications may seem rather frivolous or unnecessary. The Maestro makers are proud enough of their computerized hatchback, though some of us may have reservations about a synthetic voice that exhorts us on proper courses of action. Of course, the on-board computer carries out a number of functions (for example, it analyses fuel consumption), but the fact that the computer voice can offer dire warnings has been the feature to attract most attention. There is also something of a mystery as to why particular types of voices have been selected. Models for the British and French markets are graced with a *female* voice, whereas Maestros destined for Italy and Germany come equipped with a *masculine* voice. We may speculate on why this should be. Perhaps the explanation is the simple one that has been offered, that a woman sounded better in English and French. The actress Nicolette McKenzie, the woman behind the voice, observed: 'When I did the tapes I aimed to project a calm voice appealing to both men and women.'

The Computerized Car

The fancy talking computer in the relatively recent Maestro should not make us forget that computers have lurked in motor cars for many years. One important impulse behind this development was legislation – relating, for instance, to pollution – in the United States. By 1978, American car manufacturers were including microprocessors in their products for many different reasons. There were micro-tuned radios, micro-tuned instrument panels and micro-controlled information systems. The Cadillac Seville Trip Computer not only told the driver where he was going, and whether his fuel was sufficient for the journey, but also told him when he had arrived. The early Chrysler Electronic Lean Burn system was used to control ignition timing, and Ford's Electronic Engine Control, the EEC-11, was one of the first systems that came close to meeting the stringent air-pollution standards set for the early 1980s. Computerized cars may not all be vehicles like in 'Knight Rider', but computers in cars have been around for some time.

Controlling Vehicle Suspension

Sometimes computer facilities are present where we least expect them. They can be used, for example, in conjunction with shock absorbers. Both Cadillac and Buick have offered a suspension feature that combines analogue electronics with a simple silicon chip. General Motors has introduced the Automatic Level Control for rear suspension, a system designed some years ago by Delco Electronics and Delco Products. The device employs an Optron diode sensor to measure the distance from the axle to the frame; then, controlled by the analogue and logic circuits, it adds or subtracts compressed air from a 150-psi supply in the shock absorber configuration to adjust the level of the rear of the vehicle.

Computerized Roads

Computers are finding their way on to roads for various purposes. They can be used, for example, to monitor bus arrivals and departures, to control the scheduling of commercial freight systems, to control traffic lights to minimize congestion in towns and cities, and to supervise the collection of tolls. Computers, we know, can aid the design of roads and bridges, just as they can influence the design of aircraft and ships. Transport by road, as with transport by air or water, is scarcely a credible option in the developed world without the multi-faceted involvement of computer-based systems. As one example, a combined Driver Aid and Toll Registration system is in operation in New South Wales in Australia. The system controls motorway 'lanterns' and switches emergency telephones through to a central office. And the computer, an Argus 700E, also monitors motorway instrumentation such as vehicle counters. When toll information is collected, statistical reports are automatically printed out at the central office.

The Computerized Railway

As with airlines, computers can be used to book passengers on to trains. And it is possible to automate freight monitoring, the arrival and departure of trains, information displays, and the generation of timetables. Track sensors can be monitored to provide safety controls, and internal services – entertainment, food and drink, advice, etc. – can be computer-controlled. Many aspects of train operation throughout the world are now automated, and it is inevitable that the trend will continue. Train power-consumption can be monitored for energy conservation purposes. Revenue can be collected automatically, and information stored to aid the planning of future programmes involving financial investment. Again, we may expect a robot-driven train to meet psychological resistance from passengers – and from staff likely to lose their jobs!

Computers on the APT

The Advanced Passenger Train (APT) faced a variety of problems, and perhaps some of them were connected with computers. One use of micros on this unlucky vehicle was in providing a speed advisory system (C-APT) to help the driver of the train maintain the correct speed at all times – once they could get the thing moving, that is. The micro-based C-APT system received information relating to line speed from devices in the track along the route of the train. The positions of the devices (called 'transponders') had been carefully worked out to take into consideration a number of factors, such as line-speed limit, train braking characteristics, and the need for the system to exhibit 'fail-safe' features. A paper describing the advisory system concludes that the decision to use microprocessors in this application was the correct one, so perhaps we can't blame computers for the lamentable history of the APT.

Testing for Track Cracks

British Rail, always keen to adopt new technology, has employed arrays of microprocessors to check at least some of the 20,000 miles of railway track in the United Kingdom. Equipment developed at Harwell comprises fourteen Intel 8080 micros, a minicomputer, and other electronic bits and pieces. The system allows data about cracks to be processed as the train is running, thus cutting out the former laborious laboratory processing. Cracks are instantaneously indicated by an alarm signal, with a splash of paint being ejected on to the track to act as a marker. The test-train is required to run at about 25 m.p.h., with ultrasonic probes gliding over the rails on a layer of water. We are urged not to confuse this technique with a more complicated method that allows flaws in track geometry to be detected when the train is travelling at up to 120 m.p.h.

Micro for a Bum Job

Rumour has it that British Rail used to employ people with sensitive bottoms to test the comfort of train rides, and so aid the design of suspension and other equipment. A year or so ago, however, such obliging folk were abandoned and British Rail – in a spasm of technological innovation – turned to the microcomputer. Kemo of Beckenham designed a system using a micro and accelerometers which was employed to test for passenger comfort on the ill-fated Advanced Passenger Train. The equipment in question, about the size of a shoe-box, contains two separate accelerometers to measure forwards and sideways movement, and a microcomputer to process the resulting information. Readings can be taken in two ways, one of which detects the sorts of vibrations that can cause travel sickness. Data from the tests can be used to build up comfort (or discomfort) curves for comparison with curves on motion sickness data produced by the International Standards Organization.

Computerized Ports

Now that we know about airports, railways and roads, it is no surprise that computers are used at ports, often for very similar purposes. There are, for instance, automated port facilities for traffic control, traffic monitoring, electricity monitoring and control, freight monitoring, displays to indicate shipping status, customs, etc. An Argus 400 computer system is used as an information and booking system at Dover Harbour, one example among many. The Argus services television monitors and keyboards located at vehicle checkpoints, and also controls the large-character display boards in public transit areas and car parks. Harbours and ports would be grossly inefficient in the modern world without the assistance of the digital computer.

Saving the Sailors

A set of twelve British coastal radio stations has linked up with a computerized base in the United States, to monitor the positions of about eight thousand ships around the world. The Automated Mutual-Assistance Vessel Rescue system (AMVER) enables the rescue authorities quickly to ascertain the position of any ship in trouble and the locations of other merchant ships in the area which may be able to render assistance. AMVER has worked successfully for many years, but increased computerization has rendered the systems more efficient. Coastguards in Britain can locate ships more quickly, and by 1980 more than half of all British merchant ships were participating in the system.

Saving the Yachtsman

The yachtsman Richard McBride ran his schooner aground in East Falkland in March 1983. He owed his life to a weather satellite and the associated computer-based data-processing facilities. Each boat in the race in which he was participating carried a small transmitter which passed information to a weather satellite operated by the French Space Agency and the American Weather Agency. It was by means of this device that McBride was tracked down. But in the years to come, this service may not be available. Europe's two Meteosats are expected to run out of fuel in the next year or two, and the United States is considering withdrawing one of its two polar-orbiting weather satellites as an economy measure. Such a decision may affect the African and tropical ocean in particular, since in such regions there are few ground-based systems. Unless the US and Europe decide that the satellites are worth the considerable cost, then few may be launched in the future for purely meteorological reasons.

The Computer Yachtsman

On occasions, computers have been allowed to sail yachts. One of the first instances was when a Wang computer effectively replaced the entire crew for the 236-foot yacht *Club Méditerranée*, the second-place winner in the 1976 OSTAR race between Plymouth (England) and Newport (Rhode Island). The computer had one human companion, the skipper and computer operator Alain Colas, for the 25-day voyage. The 'crew' was programmed by Compagnie Internationale Service L'Informatique. The computer was able to stand watch continuously, a task it ably undertook by monitoring twenty-four instruments. The system was programmed not to bother the skipper with mundane information, but to provide *exceptional* information and *requested* items of data. An automatic alarm was activated by the computer whenever the humidity approached fog level, and a computer alarm was initiated if radar indicated the close proximity of another vessel. The computer also checked for unacceptable course deviations, leaking propane or hydrogen, and for overcharge of batteries by the wind-vane generator. The electronic crew was also engaged in calculating locations from sextant readings, in planning ideal courses, and in decoding and printing morse-coded weather reports.

Computers as Submariners

Controlling a submarine – particularly for experimental purposes – can be a hazardous operation. Much better to let computers do it! One of the first computer-controlled submersibles was Angus, a cable-powered vehicle successfully sea-tested in 1977 by the Underwater Technology Group of Heriot-Watt University (Edinburgh). Angus was intended to operate as a research tool to investigate new systems of propulsion, buoyancy, control, navigation and other aspects of sea-bed surveying by remotely controlled vehicles. This submersible moves at around 1 knot, scarcely the speed for a modern Captain Nemo. A main function of the underwater microcomputer is to provide a flow of control information to a computer that may be sited on a nearby ship. The computers can then converse, the control computer telling the micro what to do next.

The Robot Diver

Computer-controlled submersibles are sometimes seen as automated robot divers. The dangers of oil and gas production in deep waters have often been pointed out, and it would seem obviously desirable to automate as many underwater tasks as possible. We have already talked about Angus. One of his co-workers is the automated SMARTIE system (which stands for 'submarine automatic remote television equipment'), which is intelligent by virtue of an on-board microcomputer. In 1976 the developing company, Marine Unit Technology (Surrey, England), believed SMARTIE to be the first intelligent unmanned submersible. In this device the micro is capable of considerable local control. For example, using data from the submersible's magnetic compass and gyro, the microcomputer can project an artificial navigation target on the operator's video screen situated on a surface ship, providing the operator with guidance assistance even when the underwater visibility is zero.

The Computerized Airport

Computers are used for many specific tasks at airports (see below for details of safety measures, runway checking, wind monitoring, etc.). Today, computers book seat-reservations, check passengers in, control the handling of freight, provide information for airport staff and passengers, and maintain staff records and other files. Progressively, computers are coping with an increasing range of tasks once the province solely of human beings. We can imagine a time when people will collect their tickets from automated dispensers, have their luggage handled by robots, board a robot-controlled plane with a pre-programmed destination, and be entertained *en route* by computer-controlled entertainment centres. The blocks to this sort of total systems integration will prove to be psychological rather than technical.

The Helicopter Pilot

By 1980, people were forecasting that computers could be flying helicopters within ten years. Les Walker, contracts manager of the engine electronics division of Lucas, has suggested that the problem is more psychological than technical ('People still think electronics is magic'). The Lucas system, which has interested Bell Helicopters, replaces the pilot's controls with a push-button computer panel. Here a microprocessor is used to control the engine and in turn the rotors, seemingly easier to control than winged aircraft. Pre-programmed flights have been forecast: before you take off, you simply indicate the destination and then press a button. The helicopter takes you where you wish, automatically and in complete safety. The Civil Aviation Authority has commented that the microprocessor pilot would still be required to do two hundred hours of airborne training to get a licence – and they would never license a computer!

Avoiding Mid-air Crashes

Computers are increasingly being enlisted to make air travel safer – as, at the same time, they render cruise missiles more effective. For some years, the US Federal Aviation Administration has been developing a microprocessor-based system for avoiding airborne collisions that can be used reliably and effectively. For example, it is a good idea to avoid false alarms and interference with ground-based air-traffic control systems. One idea is that a cockpit display would show the relative positions of aircraft in the vicinity and the microprocessor would at the same time recommend optimum avoidance paths. Use would be made of aircraft antennae to scan the surrounding region, with computers rapidly analysing the results to detect potential threats. A typical system might issue only vertical manoeuvre commands (climb or dive) for collision avoidance, but more sophisticated systems will allow a more flexible range of response. Modern aircraft are already heavily computerized. It will not be long before we see pilots becoming more or less redundant cargo, possibly allowed to remain in the front of aircraft for the reassurance of passengers, but for no other reason.

Testing Icy Runways

Pilots have always worried about running out of runway when landing, because of excessive damp or ice. Some years ago the Swedish Saab-Scania company developed a system able to test runway friction. A microprocessor-controlled configuration was built into a standard Saab 99 Combi coupé. This Saab Friction Tester was able to travel fast enough to test for hydroplaning, and so received much attention from airport authorities in Europe, North America and Japan. One attraction was that the vehicle could be used for ordinary service purposes when not engaged in testing runways. The Saab system was seen as the first friction-testing device that could check for friction at high speeds and specifically at hydroplaning speeds. The system was seen as a significant development from the 'cornflake-box days', when a car would be sent out with a box of cornflakes on the passenger seat: if the box slid on to the floor when the brakes were slammed on, then aircraft were allowed to land! Computers are remarkable fellows, but some of us may be surprised to find them simulating 'sensitive bottoms' for British Rail (pp. 74–5) and cornflake packets for airport managers!

The Back-seat Pilot

Here is yet another indication that decision-making is being taken out of the hands of human pilots. This time the objective is to make aircraft fly more quietly. It seems that British Aerospace reckons that computers are better than people at reducing the amount of noise that an aeroplane makes. In British patent application 2/101/060, it is acknowledged by the company that pilots can reduce the nuisance element in aircraft noise by cutting the aircraft thrust over patterns of dense population. Alas, since the surrounding population near the world's airports varies from one location to another, the well-intentioned pilots sometimes get it wrong, boosting the power when they should be cutting it and vice versa. The answer, inevitably, is a minicomputer. Before take-off, data about relevant airports are fed into the mini, and then during the subsequent flight the computer gives the pilot signals to indicate when it is a good idea to boost the engine power or to reduce it. It will soon be even more of a mystery why the pilot needs to be there at all!

The Longer-living Aircraft

Aircraft can suffer from fatigue – with occasional tragic consequences, as James Stewart once showed us. But a microprocessor-based fatigue-measuring system, first installed in the Panavia Tornado bomber, could extend the lives of aeroplanes. The system was developed by the Croydon company Negretti and Zambra in conjunction with the Royal Aircraft Establishment at Farnborough. Naturally the device was developed for the military first, but it was soon seen to have possibilities for civil aircraft. With metal fatigue measured more accurately, it would no longer be necessary for airline operators to withdraw a whole fleet after a set period, perhaps prematurely. Aircraft could safely fly for more years. The micro-based device harnesses a new principle to measure the fatigue-producing loads: the meter is in fact an accelerometer linked to the microprocessor which measures damaging accelerations by means of the 'threshold-counting' technique. Eight levels of acceleration can be measured, a counter registering every time the plane is subjected to an acceleration which strains the structure by a set amount. Next time you fly, just keep hoping that the micro got its sums right.

Testing the Aircraft Structure

Computers are now testing aircraft frames with a new rigour. British Aerospace, among other aircraft companies, is now using a wide range of computerized test facilities to improve designs. Base Ten Systems Ltd of Farnborough have produced a data–acquisition system able to handle up to 1,280 channels of information, with use made of the MAGUS family of modules. Under the control of a minicomputer, the system can record special test data up to the moment of structural collapse; other computer programs can be used to measure the accumulated data and make interpretations to aid aircraft design. With such high–powered design technology around, why do aircraft ever fail?

Is Your Plane on Fire?

It can be useful for a pilot to know whether or not his aircraft is *really* on fire. A false alarm can have unfortunate consequences: an aircrew may, for example, bale out unnecessarily – which is unduly costly in terms of hardware and hurt pride. Inevitably, computers are improving the situation. A microprocessor-based detection system, being developed by the British firm of Graviner under a US Air Force contract, should help to reduce the embarrassment. The system will tell the pilot how serious the fire is: the aeroplane may be on fire but perhaps he should stick with it; it may not be as serious as the alarms suggest, or it may be! (But why should he trust the microprocessor if he can't trust his alarms?) Ultraviolet detectors using metal electrodes in a gas-filled capsule can detect flames at distances of up to twenty metres in ideal conditions (will the conditions be ideal?). The sensors are not troubled by solar radiation which can sometimes infiltrate high-flying aircraft. Microprocessors could be distributed in various likely places, linked to sensors and giving the pilot a range of warnings. The micro could also set off fire extinguishers in appropriate circumstances. Again, the pilot should stick around, if only to see how the fire-fighting micros are coping.

The Space Robot

The Grumman Aerospace Corporation has developed a robot beam-builder for the American space shuttle. The robot will be expected to build communications platforms, orbiting space stations, and eventually even more elaborate space structures. The 8,000-kg space robot was ground tested in the late 1970s, and is capable of producing triangular trussed beams from aluminium ribbon at the rate of one metre a minute. The ribbon is worked into V-shaped edge members for the truss, and they are braced by pre-cut struts stored on board the robot. Automatic welding is carried out. We may expect to see 'space walks' carried out by robots. Unmanned space exploration seems to be an increasingly practical option.

The NASA Teleoperator

This is a robot developed by Bell Aerospace for NASA. One objective of the device is to study the control of space vehicles from the ground. In operation, the robot moves on a smooth surface on pinpoint jets of pressurized gas, one thousandth of an inch thick (a veritable hovercraft). With friction reduced in this way, it is possible to imitate docking and other space activities. The robot was designed for installation in space vehicles to carry out a variety of tasks. It could, for example, capture and destroy orbiting satellites, service and repair spacecraft, and rescue astronauts in difficulty. Forty digital and analogue radio links will link the teleoperator to control facilities on earth.

Microcomputers in Space

Computers are now being used in a wide range of space applications. Indeed there would be no space programme – East or West – without the contribution of computers. One thing they do, after we have launched them into orbit, is control the attitude of a space vehicle. As far back as 1979, a complementary-MOS microprocessor was first used to control the disposition of a small US satellite, Magsat, launched to study the earth's magnetic field. Johns Hopkins University built the satellite and the RCA Corporation supplied the microprocessor to monitor and control the vehicle's pitch, roll and yaw. Magsat, in fact, was designed to fly like an aeroplane relative to earth, with one side facing downward 'and another oriented towards the normal of the orbit'. Various sensors – for example, an infra-red detector – were provided to feed data to the micro. And the microprocessor was equipped to decide if the sensors were providing erroneous data!

Experimentation in Space

It may not come as a surprise that computers are also equipped to run their own scientific experiments on board a spaceship. One such experiment was designed to measure the d.c. and low-frequency electric fields in the magnetosphere. This was done by monitoring the voltage between two conducting spherical probes, each of which was connected to a space vehicle by about forty metres of cable. Motors to unwind the cables were activated by computer, and data were collected and analysed automatically. The on-board Intel 8080 microprocessor needed only one watt of power. Again, the success of this type of experiment suggests that scientific research does not require men to be sent into space.

7. Machines in Industry

'It's no good. They're programmed to commit hari-kiri if you try
to discover their architecture.'

Robots to Shear Sheep

Robots seem somewhat daunting fellows when they start dealing directly
with living creatures. At the twelfth International Symposium on Industrial
Robots (Paris, June 1982), we were told that a sheep-shearing robot had been
constructed and successfully tested at the University of Western Australia.
The robot in question comprises a conventional shearing cutter mounted on a

computer-controlled, hydraulically actuated arm. A crucial element in the control program is a model of the expected shape of the sheep surface: the model is used to provide effective control of the robot movement over the sheep. Apparently, trials have shown that the initial shape of the model surface had to be modified to allow for variations in the shape of individual sheep. Electronic sensors measure the proximity of the sheep skin and so control the behaviour of the cutting head. The sheep being sheared is strapped down to prevent inconvenient – and potentially tragic – movement during the shearing process. Some discussion has already occurred as to whether sheep should be anaesthetized to render them immobile while they are being sheared by a robot.

The Computerized Factory

Many efforts are being made *totally* to computerize the factory – to arrange uninterrupted production that is largely independent of human intervention. A classic case is the Fanuc robot factory in Japan, where robots and computer-controlled machines work all day and all night – these robots don't need to see. But not all the unmanned factory production is being conducted in Japan. There are impressive efforts being developed in Europe, and it is worth mentioning the McDonnell Douglas parts fabrication plant in St Louis. Here, some two dozen acres of milling machines have been working for several years grinding grooves, slots and intricate patterns in airframe parts to a tolerance of 0.0025 inch (0.06 mm). For the most part, the machines work alone, watched by a few men who look at a control panel from time to time, and sweep the cuttings. And the men are not in charge. The machine tools are supervised by numerical controllers which in turn are controlled by a massive hierarchy of computers governed by a master computer. This type of unmanned factory is remarkable, but not unique. Other factories throughout the world are producing cars, engines, earth movers, oil-well equipment, electrical products and machine tools, with ever diminishing human involvement.

Controlling the Noisy Factory

It is now possible to find out what factory equipment sounds like to those who live in the vicinity. Scientists at Batelle's Columbus Laboratories in Ohio have recently produced a set of microcomputer programs to allow engineering firms to discover exactly how compressors, pumps, oil flares, etc., will sound to those who live near by. The programs, costing a mere $500 (in 1983), run on an Apple II computer and compute the direction and level of sound coming from as many as fifteen different sources at different locations. The various sounds are split into frequency bands in the range of the human ear, and data about each band is fed into the system. It is even possible to add background noises to make the situation more realistic. Results can be printed out as combined sound levels in one place, or as a contour map showing the decibel levels. This should make it possible to design quiet factories.

The Computer Draughtsman

Computers can produce engineering and other precise drawings, just as, in a more free-ranging mood, they can generate original 'paintings'. The production of drawings by computer is a prodigious realm. There are now plenty of computer-based plotters on the market, and these show a variety of skills for particular purposes. Benson high-speed plotters, for instance, can handle drawing sizes up to A0 and B1. Servo-motors, under automatic intelligent control, are used to drive the plotters, and the plotter pens, like robot grippers, come in various shapes and sizes. The pen may be liquid ink, ball Pentel, pressurized ballpoint or fibre tip – all in the same Benson carriage. A microprocessor provides a character set that can be drawn at any size and any angle. Drawings can be produced, to any specification, flawlessly, rapidly and repetitively. How can a (human) draughtsman compete? Programs are available, for example, for hidden line removal, scaling, windowing, rotating, projections, etc. So you see where we're at: computers can design an artefact, produce the drawings, control the manufacture of the item, and see that it is wrapped and crated. What else is there?

The Sexy Machine

Sexual activity has something to do with procreation, though people often think it is exciting for other reasons. So far, computers and robots tend not to become aroused – whatever the stimulus – but they are taking an interest in reproduction. Somewhere in *Coningsby*, Benjamin Disraeli noted that 'The mystery of mysteries is to view machines making machines.' Today it is happening. A reputable journal (*Machinery*, 3 March 1982) observed that modern machine tools are unique in that they alone, among machines, are capable of reproducing themselves: 'There is a breakthrough, the outcome of some astute genetic tinkering and brilliant husbandry by a Japanese company. Right now, a group of eighteen standard machining centres is busily producing offspring in a propagating unit where a man has been relegated to a mere observer.' And the machines don't stop for coffee breaks, cleaning up, or sleep ('At night, the reproduction cycle continues at full speed in the darkened, deserted building.'). The Yamazaki Machinery Works may not think that its machine-reproducing unit is very sexy, but the competence of the computer-controlled configuration says some interesting things about machine procreation (and see also p. 165).

Computers Build Computers I

There are various ways in which computers are evolving their own reproductive mechanisms! Computers are, for example, designing other computers – and gradually they are learning to build them also. One step in building a computer is to produce the required semiconductor circuits; and one stage in this process is to achieve effective wire-bonding. The Japanese Nippon Electric Company is developing an automated wire-bonding system to assist in the manufacture of semiconductor circuits. This robot system, computer-controlled, uses artificial eyes to carry out the necessary tasks. All this may sound pretty revolutionary but the first fully automated transistor wire-bonding system was introduced by Nippon in 1976!

Computers Build Computers II

At the IBM East Fishkill plant, sixty miles north of Manhattan, computers are making computers. Now a production line for silicon chips is almost totally supervised by computers. In a veritable factory within a factory, computer-controlled tools are sealed from an outside world contaminated by dust and human beings. The basic chip wafers arrive in sealed containers and are then floated on jets of clean air along glass-tunnelled railways. This method is used to convey the chips, the fundamental elements of all modern computers, from one production process to another. And the travel of the wafers along the tracks is monitored by computers – to avoid traffic jams. This automated production process is so speedy and efficient that an IBM engineer in Europe, say, can design a new chip on a Friday night – using design computers, of course – transmit the information by satellite to the East Fishkill computers, and have the new chip in existence by Monday morning. Again, we see how computers are involved in influencing the course of their own evolution.

Assembling Those Disk Drives

Robots are already building robots, and they are starting to build computers. Today Shugart Associates of California has successfully tested a robot performing the initial eight-step assembly process for one of the firm's disk-drive products. (Ron Albo of Shugart has observed: 'If a robot can do a job, a person shouldn't be doing it.') Assembly time for the disk drives has been dramatically reduced to less than one minute (three people formerly took two minutes to complete one disk-drive assembly). Furthermore, the robot, untroubled by fatigue and boredom, maintains the same high standard on every product. Use is made of an articulated robot arm with elements roughly corresponding to the human shoulder, elbow, wrist, hand and fingers. The fingers grasp the object, moving it first to a work-station and then to an inspection platform. The computer program, the effective brain of the system, is controlled from a keyboard. The company plans to introduce more robots, to increase productivity and reduce costs. This is a further interesting 'closing of the loop' – computers are starting to design computers, and robots are starting to assemble them.

The Computer Miner

The birth of the computer miner is largely connected with the name of Professor Meredith Thring of London University. He designed his first robot miner in the early 1970s, and his methods have been dubbed with the fancy word 'telechirics'. New breeds of robot miners are likely to look somewhat humanoid, even to the point of carrying a small television camera (superficially akin to the old miner's lamp) on their heads. People on the surface would wear helmets linked electronically to the robot cameras, and the human being could scan the underground scene simply by moving his head to move the robot head. The robot arms would be controlled in a similar fashion. The human being could move his arms while watching a television display of what the robot was seeing, and the robot could 'sympathetically' carry out the required tasks, often in hazardous circumstances, without the human being suffering any threats from the hostile environment. If Arthur Scargill doesn't want to travel from Yorkshire, then perhaps a surrogate 'telechiric' union leader could meet the Coal Board. Or is one King Arthur enough?

The Precise Robot

Robots have often had problems with their movements. Their minds might be alert and computer-fast, but their limbs have generally been sluggish and rather clumsy. You will not be surprised to learn that this is all changing. Robots are today learning to move more speedily and with greater accuracy. IBM, amongst other companies, is said to be working on robots that can move their limbs rapidly to an accuracy of less than 0.1 millimetre. Robot movements can be tracked using lasers or photogrammetry; IBM seems to favour the laser-tracking methods. One aim behind the new accurate robot species is to facilitate assembly tasks in the factory environment. For example, Philips Research Laboratories (Eindhoven, Netherlands) have developed an industrial robot called EPAAS (for Experimental Programmable Adaptive Assembly System). This fellow is said to be capable of assembling components with clearance of no more than 10 μm (one hundredth of a millimetre). The robot hand carries a camera eye, and other senses are available. Soon robots – made of metal, plastic, etc. – will be more skilled than the most dexterous human beings.

The Designing Computer

We are seeing that the computer is becoming increasingly skilled at generating good designs of a wide range of artefacts, many of which are taken for granted in modern society (elsewhere we mention shoes and buildings). In industry, computers are being used to design thousands of items – this book could be devoted solely to design applications! Here, to supplement the other design cameos, it is worth mentioning some of the design interests of the Cambridge CAD (Computer-aided Design) Centre. There are now programs available to design complex components having doubly curved surfaces, electrical circuitry layouts, distillation columns for chemical plants, tubular heat exchangers, piping systems for process control, and tank shells for storage of industrial chemicals. The list could be indefinitely extended. The computer designer is an essential factor in the modern industrial world.

Computers to Design Motors

We are not likely to be surprised to learn that computers can also design electric motors. Various universities (for instance, Warwick and Cambridge in England, and the University of Southern California) have been involved, for example, in the computer-aided design of axial-field machines. Particular research has focused on the design of a wheelchair motor.

Designing Golf Balls

We may expect computers to design bridges and aircraft, but golf balls? Golf buffs have known for well over a century that the flight of a golf ball is affected by its surface profile. The profiled surface produces aerodynamic lift, allowing a ball with surface protrusions or indentations to travel further than a smooth ball. Hand-chiselled designs have developed through the bramble or pimple pattern, and the regular lattice design, to the rounded dimples of most modern balls. Pimples tended to become flattened during play, and in lattice designs the recesses tended to collect dirt. Dimples solved most of the problems, but research has suggested that the best results are obtained with a symmetrical pattern – a ball with the greatest number of 'equators' (lines around the circumference which divide the ball into equal halves). Most conventional golf balls only have three equators. Now a computer-designed ball, the new Dunlop DDH, has ten. The computer devised a pattern composed of four different dimple sizes, arranged uniformly on the surface of the ball – and research has proved the superiority of the design. Golfers are enthusiastic, and the company is aiming to manufacture 15 million balls per annum.

Computers to Design Shoes

Today computers are helping to design almost every type of artefact – chairs, aircraft, kitchens, computers themselves . . . and shoes. Clarks's technical consultant, Tony Darvill, inspired by developments in the aerospace industry, first suggested using computers for shoe design in 1968, and today the company claims that computer-aided design has produced more up-to-date styles and shoes that fit better. The CAD Centre in Cambridge spent four years developing a system for shoe-making, exploiting the famous Polysurf program which is able to define free-form surfaces. The system's 'art module' allows a human designer to draw lines and 'paint' up to 16 million colours on a display screen! Geoffrey Egan, Clarks's development and engineering manager, has observed: 'We are trying to quantify an art and to get rid of the mystery around the shoe-making craft.'

Making That Shoe

So a computer has designed a shoe! Now, how does the computer set about manufacturing it? One task is to map a curved surface on to a plane: the shoe material starts off flat but it will not finish up that way. The upper and insole of a shoe are cut from sheet material (leather, poromeric, plastic-coated fabric or whatever), which is then shaped to form the curved surface that will enclose a male or female foot. The pattern for a component can be regarded as a plane map of the corresponding portion of curved surface. Interestingly enough, shoe-makers and map-makers face the same problem – they both have to solve the problem of the relationship between flat concepts and curved realities. Curve theory is immensely complicated and can involve multi-dimensional space and the use of isometric trees. Suffice it to say that computers now know how to translate a curve requirement into a flat pattern to be cut. This remarkable insight allows computers to make aircraft components, as well as shoes. Perhaps God used isometric trees and a handy computer when he made curved planets and curved people!

Computerized Carpet Dyes

Computers are now controlling jets of dyes to produce reasonably cheap carpets with good designs. Before 1980, the Carpet Manufacturing Company of Kidderminster (England) had spent nearly £4 million developing a computer-based system following an idea of the Austrian inventor Peter Zimmer. In the Chromotronic process adopted by the company, dye is applied by means of high-pressure jets which are small and tightly focused. This approach achieves a sharpness of pattern and depth of colour akin to that in more expensive woven carpets (the company is making carpets that are considerably cheaper than woven versions). The carpet is passed under eight dyeing heads, each of which can carry as many as four hundred dyeing jets. The jets, under computer control, are switched on and off, according to how they are intended to contribute to the overall pattern. The pattern can be changed simply by changing the tapes that control the computer. The carpet moves through the process at a rate of three metres per minute, and the production line for the carpet is no less than 122 metres in length.

Stock Control of Yarn

Computers can be used to control stock in any field, whether we need to keep track of pills, nuts and bolts, lumps of rubber, cans of food, bales of cloth, car parts, etc. The knitting industry for example, has not been slow to make use of microcomputers for inventory control of yarn. A Leicester company, the Leicester Computer Centre Ltd, is marketing a 'Yarn Stock Control' program to help small knitting firms. And the program even generates reports – a yarn-usage report, a yarn-movement report, etc. – to tell managers what they should do next. The program, running, for example, on an Apple II microcomputer, is reckoned to be cheaper and quicker than any 'normal' system.

Compute-a-suit in Finland

The Truro company in Kuopio, Eastern Finland, is using computers to design suits, cut the cloth, and automatically convey material from one site to another. In consequence, we are told, productivity is rising and Truro has been forced to think 'more precisely' in all its management decisions, from product planning to cloth buying. The human designers specify their wants on display screens and then the computer-controlled printer-plotters trace out the dimensions at full scale. One massive printer-plotter is said to 'scream like a banshee' (a Finnish banshee) as it races over the paper. The necessary information is then transferred to the cloth-cutting computers which calculate the shortest route from one cut to the next. Next time that new suit doesn't fit, don't blame the tailor – there probably isn't one!

Planning That Chemical Plant

Chemical plants can be unsightly, and the neighbours may not like new plans for plant construction. The Cambridge CAD Centre has developed a new way of finding out what a new chemical plant will look like once it is built. The computer is fed with a mass of constructional details, and it then generates a display showing the appearance of the plant. Photographs – three-dimensional and in full colour – can be taken from the display screen, and this can aid public inquiries concerning the erection of new plant. The computer-generated pictures can also be superimposed over pictures of the local environment to indicate the scenic effects if the plant were to be built. Who, however, would have the last word? Picture aids are one thing, democratic influence another.

The Computer Energy-saver

Computers can be enlisted to save energy in homes and factories. In fact, it is now essential for factory plant managers, particularly in the United States, to computerize their energy-control provisions. Energy costs and legislation compel such an approach. Computers can be used to supervise lighting levels, internal factory temperatures, machine control, etc. In one *manually* controlled system, a human operator forgot to switch off selected equipment during a thirty-minute period. The result was an additional $20,000 in demand charges. The attractions of reliable computer control are not difficult to see. In 1972, a US department-store chain introduced IBM System/7 computers in a main store, and within a few years the system was controlling lighting in no less than twenty-four stores across three states. By the late 1970s, annual savings were running in excess of $750,000.

The Robot Glass-grinder

Unimate robots are now helping the manufacture of windows for motor cars. In one successful application, two 2000B robots load and unload automatic grinding machines for glass edges. The maximum glass size for these robots is 28 × 68 in. (71.1 × 172.7 cm). Each robot has a special double hand so that a finished part can be deposited on an output conveyor as a new piece is picked up for machining. The hand comprises dual vacuum cups mounted back to back and with a swivel motion. This type of application has proved to be immensely profitable. The robots feed a machine that grinds the windows, and the process is unending and seemingly effortless. Each Unimate robot, it is reckoned, replaces two workers per shift on a three-shift basis. Robots can handle glass, just as they can handle metal, wood, bales of rubber, cloth and other materials. But it is not clear what the redundant workers are expected to do.

The Robot Warehouseman

Robots are tireless, patient and unlikely to insist on tea-breaks. They can be used on the factory floor, on the sea-bed, in space, for domestic work, etc. They can also be used in warehouses, to transfer materials from one location to another and to service requests for components and raw materials for assembly or machine-cutting operations. The robot warehouseman is equipped to load and unload conveyors, to palletize and depalletize, to transfer items from one handling system to another. The robot in this environment can cooperate with the robots that tend the automated machines used to cut metal. Already, fixed-path equipment has been automated for warehouse use, but the robot offers new levels of flexible operation. It is significant, for instance, that many warehouses have a constantly shifting mixture of products. Intelligent robots – with mobility and a range of senses – may be expected to cope with this situation.

Robots to Feed Conveyors

In many manufacturing processes it is necessary to feed components on to a conveyor belt for transport to the next stage of manufacture. Robots are carrying out transfer tasks of this sort for many different types of manufacturing operation. In one typical application, a robot is being used to transfer 72-lb. engine heads from an assembly conveyor to a continuously moving monorail conveyor at a major automotive manufacturing configuration. The conveyor carries a positioning shuttle to locate the cylinder head in the right position for the robot. Variations in line-speed have been found to present no problems to a robot. Robots working in such a fashion easily demonstrate their reliability and resilience. This application is dubbed 'conveyor-line tracking' – there are many examples of it in the factory world. Again, what does it say about the future of the human factory worker?

The Computer Instrument

Computerized instruments are increasingly regarded as an essential link between the human observer and a process to be monitored and controlled. In such areas as process control, power generation, chemical pathology and biomedical engineering, it is the power of the computer that enables human beings to stay aware of what is going on and of what action needs to be taken. The computer is speedy, sensitive and reliable. More and more, we dull-witted human beings rely on the computer to enhance our intelligence and perceptions.

Robots Handling Rubber Parts

The manufacture of elastomer rubber parts has traditionally exposed human beings to noxious fumes and to temperatures in the order of 400° centigrade. To unload parts from injection moulding machines, it was necessary for a person to enter the manufacturing region to strip the part from the mould. Frequent relief operators were required to ensure that no single individual was exposed to the oppressive conditions. Now you've guessed it – a robot has changed all that! In one application, a Unimate robot is being employed to unload parts from two Farrel injection moulding machines. The special robot hand – an air-operated mechanical gripper – enters the open press, strips the part from the die (using vacuum and mechanical methods), and removes the part from the press. The rubber parts are moulded two at a time, so the robot carefully places the parts over a cutting blade to separate them. When this is accomplished, the robot deposits the parts on a conveyor. Production is faster – and human operators are fired.

Hoist That Bale

The manipulation of rubber bales has been largely automated at Firestone Rubber in Orange, Texas. A Unimate robot is being employed to 'man'-handle 75-lb. rubber bales into shipping containers. First, automatic conveyors are used to transport the bales to the packaging and shipping area. Then the bales are automatically wrapped in plastic film, after which they are delivered to the Unimate robot. The robot is equipped with a special hand to transfer the bales from the two conveyors into the appropriate containers. The hand uses various vacuum facilities, and it is even arranged for the vacuum cups to puncture the plastic film so that the vacuum will not rupture it. Again, robots are good at staying the pace: rubber manufacture is, at its most economic, a seven-days-a-week operation. It has been found that manual handling of plastic-wrapped bales by human staff brings many problems. Robots offer to do the job efficiently, tirelessly, and without the threat of personnel problems.

A Computer to Test Welds

Today the welding robot is commonplace in car-manufacturing plants and other places. Once a weld has been automatically made, it can be automatically tested, with one computer-based system checking on the performance of another! The Rubery Owen company in the UK, exploiting research findings at the University of Aston, is employing a computer-controlled system to maintain the quality of spot welds. A DEC computer checks various factors, once the system has been supplied with data from the welding heads. One task is for the computer to interpret the incoming information, comparing its findings with tolerance information stored in its own memory. If the welding sequence starts to produce consistently unsatisfactory results, the computer will (metaphorically) declare 'enough is enough!' and bring the welding process to a halt. The computer informs the foreman of the action taken and provides an explanation. The foreman then decides, with computer assistance, of course, what action to take.

Finding Those Cracks

Cracks can occur in all sorts of things – and can be a problem. Now we find that computers are becoming crack-conscious, and so are becoming able to help us detect imperfections and dangers resulting from faulty artefacts. A milk bottle may be cracked, as may an aircraft wing. One type of crack is more dangerous than another, but it is not a bad idea to be able to find cracks wherever they occur. A variety of techniques – X-rays, ultrasonics, eddy currents, electrical conductivity, magnetic properties, infra-red radiation, etc. – have been exploited to discover cracks, but visual examination is often the best method. Cracks in different types of substances have different characteristics: in glass, for example, cracks can be seen as both light and dark streaks, whereas in rubber or plastics the substance may have to be flexed before a crack can be discerned. At the University of Wales Institute of Science and Technology, a filtering technique called SPOTDE has been developed to detect narrow dark streaks. The technique lends itself to computerization. So computerized crack-detection may become increasingly important for a wide range of safety and cosmetic purposes. Computer 'eyes' can already detect scratches and spots; now they are becoming familiar with cracks (see p. 74 for detection of cracks in railway tracks).

Watching Industrial Components

We are seeing the use of artificial vision in a growing range of industrial applications. We find that robots are evolving a capacity for sight and other senses. The artificial eye will soon be commonplace in factories, streets (for surveillance purposes) and the home. A recently introduced industrial system is SCAMP (Six hundred group Computer-Aided Manufacturing Project). The system includes a lighting unit, a camera, and various computer-based facilities. A robot is employed to place a part on an indexing table ready for detection and orientation by the automatic device. In fact, the robot tells the vision system that the part is present and needs attention. The vision system first identifies the form of the component and then works out which of the various similar components is actually present. This means that SCAMP is unusually bright for artificial vision systems: it can distinguish between parts that have the same silhouette, but whose internal features vary.

Checking Aerosols

The idea of using a propellant to discharge the contents of a container was first described in 1889, and today aerosol sprays find many applications – for example, perfumes, hair lacquers, insecticides, disinfectants, lubricating oils, adhesives, paints and polishes. It is hardly surprising that the necessary spray characteristics vary from one application to another: an anaesthetic spray, for example, which left untouched islands of sensitive skin would not be popular with patients, but untouched regions may be less critical for other spray applications. Now computer-based systems are available to enable spray performance to be monitored so that optimum spray features can be achieved. For instance, an interactive image analyser called AUTOVIEW has been used to inspect sprays. It includes computer programs to allow pictures of sprays to be examined. A spray can be illuminated and photographed, after which its main features can be explored. Does the spray, for example, contain large globules? Is the spray front evenly distributed? What can be said about the spray cone angle? Answers to these and other questions facilitate the design of efficient sprays for industrial and other purposes.

The Robot Painter

We have seen, in connection with artificial intelligence, that computers can produce 'paintings': these are the artistic efforts beloved by imaginative programmers. There is, however, a more practical side to computer-controlled painting – namely, the systematic and often repetitive painting of production-line artefacts in the factory environment. Robots have long been engaged in this sort of activity. For example, the first DeVilbiss Trallfa robots were installed in spray-painting applications as early as 1969, since when, on one estimate, they have clocked up well over one million working hours in industry. Spray painting, in fact, has many aspects, from coating plastic articles to undersealing motor cars. This is useful stuff, but I don't think there is yet a domestic robot to paint the house!

Robots to Thread Wires

Robots are now dexterous enough to thread wire on cable harnesses for electrical machinery. This skill – the ability to weave in and out between pegs – has been likened to the capacity of a skateboarder constantly dodging to avoid obstacles. At Lansing Bagnall (Basingstoke, England), the robot carefully pulls a piece of wire in its hand, and when enough wires have been threaded the robot neatly tapes them together. Furthermore, the robot is even equipped to position the pegs in the board before the threading starts, and to remove the pegs at the end of the operation. This work is important since cable harnesses are widely used – in vehicles, electric fires, cookers, etc. The robot 'weavers' are also dauntingly efficient. One estimate is that a robot doing this sort of job could get through as much work as can eight experienced people. The redundant people may not mind too much: they are apt to get bored, and also to scrape their hands on the pegs during the threading process. Robots are psychologically more robust and physically hardier!

The Robot Cleaner

There are a few robots that can dust furniture and scrub floors, but they tend to be fancy fellows, nicely experimental but too expensive to find their way into everyone's home. In industry, however, cleaning parts is already being performed by robots on a commercial basis, and it is likely that this type of usage will increase in the years to come. The UK Amenco company has been developing the idea of using robots for industrial washing operations, in order to fill a gap in the component washing field. Robots are better at this sort of thing than the traditional automated washing lines (which tend to be restricted to only one type of component per line). The Amenco washing centre makes use of a DeVilbiss Trallfa paint-spraying robot (robots are versatile fellows). The adapted robot sprays a mixture of detergent and water, and another nozzle blasts away the surplus detergent and any swarf that may be hanging about. A third nozzle delivers heated air to dry the (by now) clean component. Another approach is to use two robots in tandem – one to wash and the other to dry (now, where have I come across this sort of arrangement before?). The trouble is, such a set up would cost around £110,000. It won't catch on in the kitchen.

Check That Fastener

By 1980 Rockwell International had introduced a computer-controlled fastening system. Here a microprocessor was used to control pneumatic tools employed to tighten up threaded fasteners. It is important in such a mechanized system that the fastener not be tightened beyond its yield point. The system can achieve tension accuracy to a tolerance of less than 3 per cent. One consequence of this innovation is that fastener requirements could be calculated more precisely and there was no longer the need for 'engineering overkill'. This in turn led to smaller and fewer fasteners in some applications. But this technique isn't quite as easy as it sounds. The Rockwell LRM (Logarithmic Rate Method) fastening system is required to solve more than sixty equations and ninety subroutines during typical tightening cycles. Did you ever think it was so complicated to tighten a nut?

The Imaginary Lathe

Not so very long ago, if you wanted to test the operation of a workshop lathe it was necessary to try out the machine in practice. This is no longer the case. Today it is possible to 'simulate' lathe operations using computer graphics, a procedure that allows alternative methods of machining to be examined before any *real* cutting takes place. This, of course, avoids damaged tools and wasted material. The CAD Centre at Cambridge has developed the Automatic Lathes Estimating System to meet a variety of machining needs. At one stage of the operation, you feed in details of the component you want to machine: then you theoretically test out the various ways of achieving the desired shape. The most effective lathe operation can be discovered before a single sliver of metal is cut.

The Imaginary Crane

Through a host of fancy simulation techniques, computers are becoming very good at imagining things. They can, for example, imagine a working crane, to make life easier for offshore crane operators who have been forced to struggle to unload heavy equipment in rough seas. Now the operators can watch computer graphics on a screen. Researchers at Atkins Research and Development in Surrey have produced a system that can show a crane barge's movements on the sea as animated diagrams on a screen. The lift superintendent is provided with a control panel to enable him to shift ballast around in the vessel to allow compensations to be made for the vagaries of wind and tide. Thus he can be sure that the capacity of the crane will not be exceeded. Movement of the barge can dramatically increase the load on a crane, especially when a weighty piece of drilling equipment is hanging from it. The system uses a Digital Equipment minicomputer and a Sigma Electronics graphics display. The computer-based configuration, termed the 'Offshore Motion Simulator', is likely to make for safer and speedier operations on the high seas.

The Robot Laser Cutter

One fascinating development in modern technology is how frontier research in seemingly unrelated areas is combining to produce startling innovations. For example, the Scunthorpe company, Flexible Laser Systems, has now married a 400W laser to an industrial robot. The laser beam is reflected along a series of ten mirrors mounted alongside the arm's joints, before being focused with a zinc selenide lens. The system, known as 'Cobra' uses a Ferranti carbon dioxide laser, and the configuration can cut, trim, weld and even drill holes in a variety of materials. Moreover the beam can be angled to leave a clean edge on the work-piece. Cobra is one of the new breed of artificial artisans to find itself operating on a shop floor for the benefit of human beings. How does it feel about it?

Robot to Read and Assemble

Professor Yoji Umetani at the Tokyo Institute of Technology has frequently drawn attention to experimental robots being developed in Japan for a wide range of different purposes. For example, he has highlighted a remarkable Hitachi robot that is able to look at an engineering blueprint, to understand what the sketch means, and then to assemble parts according to the specification. In such a system, an electronic eye would scan the drawing, its significance would be interpreted by a computer brain, and the eye would again be used — possibly in conjunction with touch sensors — as the robot gripper manipulated parts for assembly purposes. A mobile robot with such powers would surely seem a bizarre creature on the factory floor!

Another Dexterous Robot

At the Autonetics Marine Systems Division of Rockwell International (California), a robot is now removing minute particles and pre-assembling navigational gyros with 'humanly impossible' accuracy. The robot is designed to move in five axes. It can work in a pressurized atmosphere of filtered nitrogen and can handle pressurized liquid Freon. The robot, with its effective microcomputer brain, can perform in about fourteen minutes what took human beings hours or even days. The new robot is superior to most others on the market (other models did not meet the precision cleaning requirements — the new device has been dubbed 'Mr Super-Clean'). This is yet another sign that robots are evolving the degree of dexterity formerly the sole province of *human* fingers.

Robots to Fit Car Wheels

We all know that robots weld and paint in the factory environment. And they are also learning to do many other things. In the KUKA robot plant (Augsburg, West Germany), for example, an automatic wheel-assembly system, using two IR 601/60 CP robots, has been developed. The wheels arrive on conveyors, and bolts are fed down chutes (sensitive bolt-tightening equipment is supplied by Desoutter). One of the robots is used to handle the left side of the car, while the other works on the right side. A vision system – robot eyes – is used to detect the positions of the holes in the brake-drums and to feed appropriate information to the robots. The robot then picks up a wheel and rotates the multi-bolt runner so that the holes in the wheel align with those in the brake drum. The fasteners are then automatically inserted and tightened up to a specified torque. It is interesting that the wheel hubs have to be painted white – the Bosch high-resolution camera cannot see black!

Robots Assembling Motors

The Japanese company Fanuc, in what has been hailed as a 'dramatic' move, has moved to the robot assembly of a range of servo-motors. Computer-controlled systems are used to machine the motor components and then robots set about putting the bits and pieces together. In the plant in question there are 101 robots – fifty-two in the machine-shop and forty-nine engaged on assembly activities. About sixty human beings work alongside the robots, though we may expect this number to diminish as automation advances. In some of the robot lines, the tooling needs to be changed from time to time for different products, but other lines can adapt to fresh products without retooling or reprogramming. The robots carry out a variety of assembly tasks: they manipulate oil seals, rotors and shells, fit bearings, fasten nuts and washers, etc. In 1983 it was predicted that in three years' time the factory would be totally unmanned. Robots are already carrying out simple wiring jobs. For instance, a robot can pick up a wire and place it on the correct terminal, whereupon another robot moves across to solder the wire into position.

Assembling Electric Motors

Now robots can assemble a wide range of intricate machinery. For example, a 1982 glossy brochure from the Department of Industry shows a Unimation PUMA robot assembling the rotor in a small electric motor. The assembly station is at the National Engineering Laboratory, and is part of an on-going research programme. Once a system has been designed to assemble rotors, it can be adapted to assemble other items. The computer programs include error-recovery routines, so that if the robot fails to assemble a part it will dump it and select another, rather than simply getting confused and ceasing to function. The NEL system aims to run on a single shift, after which reprogramming is necessary if fresh components are to be assembled. By 1983, motors were already being assembled at a rate of one every fifty-four seconds. This rate of production has been aided by some redesigning of motors. An assembly scheme at Westinghouse is more ambitious: here the robots are intended to switch independently from one type of assembly to another, without the need for reprogramming. Robots so conceived are able to exercise their own judgement and to take independent decisions.

Robots Assembling Cars

Robots have been busy welding cars for many years. Only relatively recently, however, have they turned their talents to the physical assembly on individual components. Mitsubishi Motors, for example, is now using some robotic devices for this sort of purpose. In one application, the robot lifts the battery from a store to a position just above the body. At the same time, a robot is used to move the front seats of the car into the vehicle. Robots, either side of the assembly line, travel along angled rails. A robot lifts the seat by squeezing the cushion in a large gripper, then it moves along the rail, tilts down slightly, and then turns to insert the seat. This type of operation is a further obvious step towards fully automatic production. Wheels are already fitted using semi-automatic equipment, and nuts are tightened by automatic machines. The human worker on the car assembly line will become an increasingly rare production element.

Robots in Nuclear Power

Everyone knows that nuclear power stations are potentially hazardous (one has only to recall what has happened at Sizewell, Three Mile Island and other nuclear power plants), though soothing noises are often made by officialdom. One acknowledged problem is how necessary work – repair, maintenance and decommissioning – can be conducted in an environment likely to be heavily radioactive. Robots are now being designed for this purpose. For example, Taylor Hitec, a small engineering firm near

Manchester (England) is designing robots that will roam around inside the next generation of advanced gas-cooled reactors and possibly inside the pressurized-water reactor due to be built at Sizewell. A 'robot on stilts' is also being designed which will be equipped to demolish nuclear power plants when they have reached the end of their lives. Robots inside the reactors will be able to carry television cameras and ultrasonic probes to relay information to operators in a safe control room. The robots will also be able to pick up items for future inspection. One of the Taylor Hitec devices will be able to manoeuvre just like a human arm. It is likely that the robots will be used in other hazardous places as well, such as chemical plants.

The Mobot Robot

This is a mobile robot developed by Hughes Aircraft and built in 1960. The aim was to develop an effective robot system for work in hazardous areas, for example, in regions contaminated by radioactivity. The robot came equipped with soft inflated pads on its hands to enable it, with variable pressure, to grasp delicate objects. Television cameras and microphones at the robot wrists provided the human operator with necessary information. Its flexible arms could move 180 degrees in any direction at each of three joints, and each arm was 6 feet long and could lift 25 lbs. Mobot could be controlled by radio or by computer, and carried one hundred command channels. Instructions were fed to the robot on tape. The Mobot torso resembles a black box from which sprout the various limbs and camera supports. Despite its flexible competence, Mobot did not have an anthropomorphic appearance. Not at all the sort of creature to become emotionally attached to.

Computerized Estate Agents

Less than 25 per cent of estate agents use computers, though 'things are starting to move': computers are learning the estate agent's trade. Two of the top-selling programs are aimed at the larger multi-branch agencies, and some local agents are prepared to pool resources to share a computer. A system from Geest can cost upwards of £5,000 for the software alone, and systems from Applied Systems Techniques (AST) start at around £10,000. There are, however, various cheaper packages: one from Cyderpress costs £850 (in mid–1983). Computers may not yet be fully competent estate agents, but it is easy to imagine a scenario in which people simply register their house details, when wishing for a sale, and the information can then be easily accessed, without the need for 'middlemen', by house hunters.

The Computerized Bookshop

Sometimes people go to book shows to look at computers! At the recent London Book Fair, Applitek was pleased to note the number of visitors to its stand, keen to see its computerized bookshop system, called BORIS and described in the handout as 'a sort of mechanized Jeeves'. Applitek shared a small stand with Teleordering, enabling booksellers to see the compatibility of the systems. Applitek has successfully demonstrated its Book Order and Inventory System, and it hopes to introduce a new stock–control package in late 1983. There is more to book shows than books!

The Computerized Architect

There is an idea that the most skilled people – the 'professionals' – will be immune to the inroads of computers. Alas, it is not true. Even fault diagnostic engineers are being replaced by computers in the field of electronics. And architecture may well become another troubled area because of the growing competence of computer programs. Not long ago, Leeds Polytechnic introduced new software, the Architectural Modeller's Toolkit, with the idea of bringing computing to the world of building design. The program was designed under a Science Research Council Grant, and use was made of a Data General Nova computer. This system can build up three-dimensional perspectives from geometric sites and buildings, and the resulting models can be used to facilitate computer-aided design. Computers can design buildings just as well as they can design shoes and electrical circuits.

The Computerized Newspaper

We all know that computers are widely used to help in the production of newspapers: for instance, computerized typesetting has caused more than one industrial-relations problem. Perhaps more remarkably, we could call up newspapers electronically on a home terminal. Imagine it: you are wakened in the morning by an electronic (but dulcet) voice which inquires whether you want to see a daily newspaper. You make your choice and the front page of the *Guardian* or the *Daily Mail* flashes up on your wall screen. Bored by dreary news of royalty and rape you intone 'Turn' – and page two appears . . . and so on and so forth. In the words of *New Scientist* (13 May 1982), 'All the technology is available, if you can afford the price of putting it together.' And the other question is – would it be worth it? The scheme may save a few trees, unless of course you decided, upon reflection, that you would like your attached printer to produce a hard-copy version of the rape item.

First You Make the Chocolates . . .

Cadbury's and other large chocolate-makers are moving steadily towards automating more and more phases of the manufacturing process. To make chocolate fillings, for instance, a microprocessor-controlled system has been installed to check the flow of about eight basic ingredients – such as glucose, cream, and a fruit mix – into a vat. The ingredients are then cooked in controlled pressure and temperature, and flavourings are also added under computer supervision. Fluid fillings are then fed to storage containers from which they are poured into chocolate shells. To change the filling, the engineer simply alters the 'software' recipe by pressing a few keys on the control console. By means of microprocessor control, a more consistent quality of product has been achieved, with a significant improvement in productivity. And once the basic chocolate has been made, it is necessary to decorate it . . .

... Then You Box Them

Once the chocolates have been decorated it is a good idea to package them, and this too is being automated. By the early 1980s, mechanical arms were putting chocolates in boxes at Cadbury's Birmingham factory. Twelve pairs of arms, using vacuum grippers, are used to pick up the chocolates and place them carefully in the plastic trays that move past on a conveyor belt. Each pair of arms is programmed to pick up just one kind of chocolate (so far there have been no demarcation disputes), and a complete tray is filled by sending it past the twelve pairs of arms in sequence. The robot arms don't always operate perfectly: on occasion a chocolate can be placed slightly askew in a box, and a human being is required to straighten the item. The German firm Otto Hansel provided the twenty-four arms, which can pack sixty trays per minute: now only twenty people are required, where formerly a line of forty human packers would be at work. Rowntree Mackintosh is also working to automate chocolate packaging by means of flexible robot systems.

The Computerized Chicken

From factory farming we look likely to be moving to automated-factory farming. A few years ago, the Japanese decided to automate their hen-houses – the Japanese don't only eat sushi! The aim was to get the hens to lay a large proportion of high-quality nourishing eggs. Sensors are employed to measure fourteen variables (for instance, temperature, humidity, the number of hens that have died, the weight of good and bad eggs, and the number of eggs produced every day). The collected information is compared with standard figures to show whether the conditions are satisfactory. The farmer can then adjust the amount of feed he gives his chickens. Mitsui and the Nippon Formula Feed Manufacturing Company initially tested the system on a number of Japanese farms. The system can quickly indicate when disease strikes the hens. It is likely that the system, so far well received (though the hens haven't been polled), will be extended to the farming of other animals, such as pigs.

The Food Maker

Japan has an answer to the hamburger – take-away sushi. And if that isn't enough, Suzumo Machinery has agreed a deal to export twenty sushi-making robots to the United States. The robots can turn out sushi – thinly sliced raw fish on top of a ball of rice – four times as fast as a skilled human sushi-maker. At the same time the Japanese are not too keen on the idea of sushi-making robots. There are sushi connoisseurs who feel that this is no place for automation through silicon chips (sushi and chips is not a popular combination in the land of the Rising Sun). One consequence is that sushi parlours have taken to hiding the robots under the counter. We may take it that the United States consumer is less fussy about who makes the sushi.

How to Sort Rice

Computers may help us to plant rice, harvest it, and sort it afterwards. The Sortex 9401 system, which includes no less than eleven microprocessors, has recently been introduced to aid the task of sorting rice. Put technically, typical inputs of American parboiled rice with a 2.5 per cent 'peck' (discoloured grains or impurities) can now be upgraded to the premium standard of 0.124 per cent 'peck', with a minimum of 'good product' present in the reject stream. And this can be achieved testing as much as 4,400 lbs. of rice every hour. The system has two operator controls: one for sensitivity and one for feed-rate. Moreover, it adjusts itself (to allow for sensitivity drift), calibrates itself (to allow for transfer from one type of rice to another), and diagnoses its own faults. Sortex 9401 can clean its own optical system, and the facility is supposed to be four times as productive as other automated sorting configurations. In brief, the system looks at the rice grains, collects data about their quality, and uses a jet of compressed air to reject imperfect ones. The rejected rice finishes up in a handy rejection bin.

Now It's the Computer Farmer

Computers are running farms, just as they are running factories. It is obvious that computers can handle all accounting and budgeting in the farm context, but they can do other things as well. The AFMS/80 system, marketed by Fullwood and Bland, can measure milk-yield, control the supply of food to cattle, and measure the body-weight and temperature of each cow. The cows carry transponders in their collars for identification purposes. One value of the computer-based system is that reports can be automatically generated to identify, for example, cows with high temperatures and cows producing a lower-than-expected milk-yield. And soon it will be commonplace to find farm computers sorting the potatoes, controlling the grain dryers, and driving tractors.

The Farming Adviser

It is now estimated that more than a thousand farmers in Britain either own a computer or have access to one. By 1983, the computer firm Comput-a-Crop (Lough, UK) was reckoning that up to 15,000 systems should be sold to Britain's 37,000 farmers over the next three years. And as many as 7,000 systems would be available for cereal crop management. In a typical system, the user is faced with a barrage of questions from the computer: has he checked rainfall? Has he counted the number of slugs per square yard? Has he investigated the growth rate of wheat? Does he know about humidity? What can he say about soil structure? Once the computer has all the information it needs, it will give advice on farming procedures. One farmer has commented that he no longer needs 'to disturb my consultant with trivial questions'. A system developed by BASF's agro-chemical division offers comprehensive cereal crop management from wheat to barley. And a Scottish farmer, Gordon Rennie, who used the computer program, was so successful achieving a yield of fourteen tonnes per hectare of winter wheat) that he earned himself a place in the Guinness Book of Records!

The Computerized Fisherman

The Japanese Sanmei company in Shizuoka has developed computerized fishing equipment. The Japanese, it seems, have an immense appetite for squid, which therefore has to be caught in ever larger quantities. In fact, half a million tonnes of more than two hundred kinds of squid are eaten in Japan every year. The delicacy can be eaten raw, pickled, dried, etc. When shredded, it is consumed along with beer. Children are said to love squid because there are no bones. Today the average Japanese fisherman is aged around fifty and there is an increasing call for automation. The Sanmei computer has been taught fishing tricks: for example, it jiggles the fishing lines to make the squid think that the bait is alive (a single line can carry as many as fifty hooks), and when the line tension caused by the catch reaches a pre-set point the computer gives the order to reel in the struggling squid. Some Japanese fishing boats now carry as many as twenty computerized units, and it is said that a boat with only eight units can catch 3,800 squid in forty minutes. Efforts have also been made to develop computers to fish for tuna and bonito – so far without much success.

Guiding the Fishermen

Another example of computers helping fishermen was demonstrated by a 1982 pilot scheme carried out by the Japan Fisheries Information Centre which set about combining data from the US NOAA-7 satellite with information from more conventional sources to draw up charts indicating where fish would probably be found. The charts were transmitted to the fleet by means of a facsimile link, which more than half of all Japanese boats carry. The experiment was reckoned to be a success: most of the boats found fish in the predicted areas. The main advantage of the scheme is that data from satellites is much more comprehensive than data from aircraft or from other surface vessels. The satellite covers Japan's 200-mile fishing-zone five times a day, and it collects information on sea temperature, cloud cover, and movements of currents. The fish may not like the new scheme, but Japanese fishermen – already pulling in 15 per cent of the total world catch – are likely to be enthusiastic.

Fishing for Tuna

It may well be that the fishing lines, computerized to catch squid, cannot be readily adapted to fish for tuna (doubtless, the day of the tuna will come). But there are other ways in which tuna fishermen have been helped by computers to increase the size of their catch. For instance, a microcomputer-driven satellite navigation system has been used to direct California tuna fishermen to better fishing areas. The system picks up signals broadcast by navigation satellites which are in a 90-minute polar orbit, and automatically calculates the ship's position. The tuna captain needs to know exactly where he is, not least because of the 1950 Tuna Conservation Act enforced from Southern California to Chile by the US authorities. If the captain evades the requirements of the Act, he may be faced with confiscation of his vessel.

Grading Fish

Once you have caught the fish, you may need to grade them. Mitsubishi Electric has developed recognition software for sorting fish – and cucumbers. The Melsort system recognizes commodities by comparing their images with features held in the computer memory. In one particular application, developed jointly with Mitsubishi Kakoki Kaisha, the system recognizes sardines, herring, anchovies and a variety of mackerel, and then grades them according to size. Ten diagrammatic elements are employed to sort the fish: these include such factors as length, width and snout shape. And what could be done with fish and cucumbers could be done with people. It would, for example, be an easy matter for computers to recognize whether a human being was male or female (think up the parameters that a sex-discriminating program would need to include).

Handling Photographic Chemicals

Some photographic chemicals are highly toxic, and it can be extremely hazardous for human beings to attempt to handle them in large quantities. Robots do not seem to mind such things and so they have been 'volunteered' for the task. Typically, highly dangerous photographic chemicals are contained in 4- or 5-quart capacity plastic bottles, which, in manufacture, are filled, capped and transferred to a location via conveyor at a rate of twenty per minute. The robot is used to transfer the bottles, two at a time, to boxes of various sizes. The robot hand and fingers are made of acid-resistant stainless steel; neoprene pads, also acid-resistant, on the fingers prevent the bottles from slipping out of position. A cassette program storage and verification unit allows the robot to behave in a flexible manner, thus enabling future product design to change without requiring a new robot-handling configuration. The Unimate robot works continuously, transferring two bottles to a box or conveyor in about six seconds. And a spillage that may seriously injure a person is ignored by the robot. What is it thinking, though?

Photographing Video Screens

There is sometimes a requirement to photograph video displays on screens, held by some people to be a very demanding task using conventional methods. Now, however, there is a computer-based system to aid the process. Polaroid has introduced the Video-Printer Model 8, a desk-top digital image processor producing full-colour images printed out from a range of computer- and video-coded signals. The device is used to convert the video signal into a digital form and to enhance highlights and shadow detail in the finished print. The many applications include satellite-data imaging, medical displays and radar weather reporting. The system is supposed to put an end to scanning lines, fuzzy edges, and those irritating reflections.

Computers as Spies

The flexibility of the modern computer brings some unexpected uses. Spying, for example, is aided by the new generation of personal computers that plug into company computer networks. This was one conclusion drawn by a gathering of international experts on computer security who met in Cannes in 1983. The proliferation of personal computers means that files of secret information are likely to be left around on a cassette or floppy disc in executive offices and homes. In such circumstances, theft is an easy matter. It may even be possible for industrial spies to plug their own personal computers into confidential data networks. Moreover, in the age of growing computer literacy, an increasing number of people are acquiring the skills to indulge in industrial espionage. Ronald Berg, of the Swedish Scandia risk-management company, observed: 'Companies can't tell you how many machines they have, so how can they possibly protect them.' Take care: someone somewhere may want to interfere with your friendly personal computer!

Computerized Big Brother

In a system being pioneered by IBM, factory workers are required to report regularly to a computer terminal. They are expected to feed in details of what work they are doing, and whether there are any problems. When the work is complete, the computer will provide the workers with instructions for the next job. The new instructions arrive on a card which the computer spews out. And it may be highly significant that the card contains instructions for both the human worker and for the numerically controlled machine tool for which he is responsible. Hence workers and NC machines are on the same level, both supervised by a computer. The IBM shop-floor terminals cost about £3,000 each (in 1983), and are linked to a foreman's office so that (human) supervisors can see what is happening. (It's nice to know that there are still human beings around somewhere.) IBM reckons that the terminals remove the need for time-and-motion men to rush round watching machines and their operators. It is significant that computers, once subordinate in all their activities to human beings, are now starting to exercise supervisory functions.

The Robot Lover

No, I don't think that robots are yet falling in love with each other or with human beings (though fiction is full of the idea). But it does appear that human beings can develop remarkable affections for robots. Not very long ago we saw a headline 'The love machine kept him at home' – and this in a quality newspaper! In this case, an industrial tribunal ordered a company to pay a man more than £3,000 for the unfair sacking of this individual. It seems he had fallen in love with a machine which had to be sent away for modernization and repair. He claimed that his own mental and physical engineering skills had been programmed into the Numerically Controlled Flame Cutting Machine – and he found it psychologically impossible to transfer to another machine. Greater love hath no man . . . At the same time, the tribunal found that he was 25 per cent to blame for the situation.

8. Offices and Administration

'Nothing to do with efficiency, Phillips. You're being replaced by something that won't smoke, spill coffee or throw up in the office'

Tory Technology

The UK Conservative Party is proud of its technology record in government, though quite another view of Tory achievement is arguable. However, the Tories do seem to have moved ahead in computerizing activities within their own party. The SDP began by computerizing its membership list – but on someone else's machine. Today, Tory Central Office, having acquired an ICL system, is able to send out mailing shots to voters in selected constituencies. And the Conservative Party rag, *Newsline*, tells us that no less than twenty constituencies have now got their own microcomputers, with another twenty actively considering the idea. One Tory agent, Hitchin's John Barrance, has observed that the Party's Clenlo Conqueror has helped speed up the call to party activists for help during elections. With the Tories drafting micros by the dozen, what's the People's Party doing?

The Democratic Computer

In various parts of the United States, France and elsewhere, computers have been enlisted to aid the democratic process. For example, people have been enabled to vote, via home terminals, on political issues. The terminals are linked to a central computer which rapidly signals the resulting vote. Viewdata was used during the 1983 General Election in the United Kingdom to poll TV audiences on election issues. Granada Television used samples of five hundred members of the electorate from all over the country. In the United States, Warner Amex set up the Qube system to allow viewers to vote after seeing politicians debate on television. And in other experiments (for example, one in Upper Arlington in the US), 'narrowcasts' of local city council meetings have been beamed to cable subscribers. With such technology, it is easy to see how an instant referendum could be organized on any issue, though whether this would be politically desirable is another matter. Futurologists are reckoned to be divided about whether the 'wired society' would reinforce or weaken democracy.

The Computer Restaurant

In the late 1970s the Orient Restaurant (Tottenham Court Road, London) decided to exploit computer technology provided by the South-West Technology company. One aim of the system was to help waiters and kitchen staff keep track of orders, prepare bills, control stock levels and carry out various related tasks. Not surprisingly, Chandru Idnani, the owner of the restaurant, has a degree in physics from London University; since 1969 he has looked at various ways of automating the catering business. Bills received by customers carry the line at the bottom, 'Bill Produced by Computer'. If Mr Idnani gets in touch with Quasar Industries he may be able to obtain some robot waiters!

The Computer Waitress

Brown's Restaurant in Oxford (England) has installed a small point-of-sale computer to cope with customers' accounts and orders (even if the order *is* 'chips with everything'). There are two terminals, one in the restaurant and the other in the bar, each with an associated printer. When the (human) waitress keys in the order, it is rapidly printed out in the kitchen. The machine adds up the amounts taken during a shift by individual waitresses. The kitchen and bar staff have been instructed to hand over goods only in response to computer orders ('The staff have confidence in the system . . . And it's very good for management control over the business.'). One consequence of the success of the enterprise is that a new venture – Brown's Computers – has been set up to sell Apple systems for small businesses. Yes, perhaps the 'computer waitress' is more a 'waitress's aid'. But we know quite enough now – about Quasar products, for example – to see how robot waitresses could cooperate with the Apple point-of-sale facilities.

The Computer Bank

The use that banks make of computers has affected us all. Anyone with an account must realize that those depressing statements are *untouched by human hand* – until you open the envelope. We now know all about automated cash-dispensing units (sometimes called automated teller machines, ATMs), and some of us may be aware of electronic funds transfer (as being practised, for example, to convey funds electronically from one bank branch to another). The trend may be towards abolishing the bank branch altogether. All you need is a means of obtaining cash (unless cash disappears too) and information about the state of your account. And, of course, there is speculation about the possibility of *home* banking. Here, you can use your bank account simply by enlisting the aid of your television screen: a console is employed to key the television into a viewdata computer system. More than one observer has suggested that the bank manager may be an endangered species – a notion which you may or may not welcome.

Watching the Pastoral Flocks

In these days of falling church attendance, it is useful to be able to keep track of the enthusiasts that remain. It may seem paradoxical to apply computer techniques to religion, but some of us may feel that believers need all the help they can get. Gareth Morgan Computer Services, based in Bristol, have recently introduced the Kubernesis Pastoral Membership System. The blurb announces: 'This is believed to be the first ever professionally developed software package for parishes and local churches in this country.' This system allows ministers and others to keep track of all those involved in the life of the church – 'to plan pastoral care, to maintain church directories, to circulate church communications, and to deal with statistics'. Gareth Morgan himself has declared that the new facility is 'a landmark in the task of churches to equip themselves for today's society'. (Of course, you knew the word *kubernesis*, so I won't bother telling you that it is the Greek term for administration in 1 Corinthians xii, 28.)

9. Watching the Environment

'*We feed the geological data for the area, the computer produces a schematic topological overview designating high probability key points, then we stick the printout on the wall and Johnson here throws a dart at it.*'

The Computer Meteorologist

Weather-forecasting, required for many different purposes, is notoriously difficult to accomplish with sufficient accuracy. Some of the largest computers in the world have been applied to this task, immensely complicated as it is by virtue of the great number of climatic and other variables. The Cray-1 computer, the largest in the world (dubbed a 'supercomputer'), is perhaps best known for its attempts to predict the weather on a global scale. The Cray-1 can carry out something like one hundred million operations every second, which gives it formidable computing power. This type of competence is essential if accurate weather-forecasting is to be useful. If a storm is to hit us in five minutes, it is not helpful if the computer takes ten minutes to work it out! The mighty Cray-1 may come to seem a veritable amateur if the current Japanese fifth-generation research plans bear fruit: the next-generation computers will be many times faster than the Cray-1 machine.

What's the Wind Doing?

It can often be useful to know how the wind is behaving. At busy airports, for instance, some knowledge of wind activity is essential for safe landings. Meteorologists at the University of Hamburg (West Germany) have developed a computer-based device that could help aircraft landing at congested airports. (And the system could also be used to track clouds of toxic waste that may arise from accidents at chemical or nuclear plants.) The SODAR (Sonic Detection and Ranging) device fires pulses of sound at winds, or patches of turbulent air, and then traps the reflected sound to compute wind-speed and direction. Airports usually know what the air is doing at ground level or very low altitudes, but they cannot erect monitoring posts above five hundred metres as these would endanger aircraft. Another problem is that a large aircraft can cause turbulence which could threaten to engulf smaller following aircraft (two light aircraft recently crashed at Reihm airport, Munich, for this reason). SODAR, now installed at various airports, make it easier to keep track of what the atmosphere is doing at any particular time.

Computers to Control Floods

Many countries have flood problems, but none more so than Holland with half its land area below sea level (in 1421, a major flood caused ten thousand deaths). Work is still going on to complete the Delta plan flood-prevention project, involving the building of massive dams in south-west Holland. A surge barrier is being constructed across the mouth of the Oosterschelde, an estuary south of Rotterdam. Computers are playing a vital part in this effort and will be directly involved in the operation of the barrier once it is complete. Computers help to provide information about weather conditions, and they are designed to control the opening and closing of the barrier. Buoys in the North Sea are 'polled' by microprocessors to provide data about rising storms, and sensors in the estuary supply further information for analysis. In such a fashion computers are helping to control the sea. It is thought that the Dutch barrier will be able to cope with any storm surge except the most calamitous that happen once every ten thousand years.

Will the River Flood?

River floods can threaten surrounding land and can jeopardize buildings near the river bank. If there is a danger of flooding, then bridge design, for example, must be able to take this into account. This can be done by using computers to simulate flooding possibilities. The US Corps of Engineers has modelled rivers by computer for some time, but traditional models have been of varying accuracy. Recently a more comprehensive model has been developed by Dr Howard Chang of San Diego State University. The model, FLUVIAL, is based on the principles of river dynamics. If you are really interested, FLUVIAL can be used to calculate three kinds of river changes: bed elevation, channel width, and lateral migration (the sideways movement of the bed within the flood-plain). FLUVIAL has been shown to be accurate by 'reconstructing' a 1980 flood that destroyed a bridge on the San Dieguito River in California. The program is thought to be particularly applicable to ephemeral streams with seasonal flooding: it can be used to aid bridge construction and urban or regional planning. FLUVIAL has been employed to improve on a failed bridge that cost $400,000!

And Not Only Flood Control . . .

Computers not only help to control floods, but also perform a wide range of other services in connection with water management. For instance, they improve water quality through control of the treatment process. They maintain consistent supplies despite fluctuating sources, and provide warning of pollution incidents. If a major disruption of supply occurs, computer control may ensure that alternative resources are rerouted. And so it goes on. Computer-controlled mechanical systems can be rendered more efficient, and so less liable to wear, and all types of equipment can be subject to constant scrutiny to ensure that no abnormal conditions exist. Ferranti computer systems, as one example, provide a range of services to the Thames Water Authority, such as ensuring that the Thames is suitable for navigation, monitoring and improving water quality, and controlling the extraction of water from boreholes. Computers are good managers – often of systems and artefacts, sometimes of human beings!

Computerized Fog Control

Various experiments have been carried out on Britain's motorways to improve the effectiveness of fog warning systems. Computer-controlled sensors at various sites have monitored the weather and other factors, such as light intensity, humidity, temperature, wind speed and rainfall, to facilitate computer analysis. The results are then displayed in police control rooms, helping the police to decide whether to switch on the fog lights, operate a convoy system, or close the motorway altogether. (Why can't the computers take the decisions?) The company Scicon developed a special language for the programs to enable computer-naive policemen to extract information from the system. We have known about computer-controlled traffic lights for a long time. Computer-controlled motorways seem a logical extension to the idea.

Watching the Oil Pollution

Now Scicon has launched a hand-held calculator version of its SCOOP (Scicon Control of Oil Pollution) program. The system can be conveniently used on the spot around the coasts and river estuaries that may be affected by oil pollution. The program has the ability to simulate the behaviour of an oil slick under real environmental conditions. The user, employing a Hewlett-Packard HP41 CV calculator, can define tidal stream, wind vector and land boundary, and can produce an appropriate stimulation of the overall pollution situation. It would be nice if the pollution didn't happen in the first place!

Computerized Sewage Control

Sewage is a nuisance – and often a health hazard. Sewage treatment needs to be reliable and efficient. Today many sewage-treatment plants are computerized. For example, the Davyhulme Effluent Treatment Works in Greater Manchester (England) has recently installed a computer-based control and supervisory system. The new facility has reduced manning levels, improved plant supervision, made it easier to expand the plant when necessary, and accomplished more efficient plant utilization. A central minicomputer is connected to eight plant-mounted telemetry out-stations, and the system accepts inputs from 263 analogue and 1,254 digital inputs to assist plant control and data logging. The first Davyhulme Sewage Works was built in 1904: a lot has happened since then.

10. Medicine and Health

'No we can't tonight Gerald, it's not safe!'

The Computer Diagnosticians

With the development of medical expert systems, immense attention is being given to medical diagnosis. One has only to think of the publicity given to such systems as MYCIN and EMYCIN. In fact, computerized medical diagnosis has been studied for many years in the context of a wide range of diseases. One writer lists fifty-eight studies in computer-aided diagnosis, which have variously focused on infective and parasitic diseases, neoplasms, nutritional and metabolic diseases, mental disorders, diseases of the nervous system and sense organs, diseases of the respiratory system, diseases of the digestive system, congenital anomalies, perinatal morbidity, diseases of the heart, etc., etc. There can be little doubt that human diagnostic competence in the field of medicine is being progressively transferred to computers. It will not be long – indeed, we are already seeing it – before we learn to trust computer physicians more than we trust their human counterparts.

Expert Medical Diagnosis

During the 1970s, increasing efforts were made to apply artificial intelligence methods to a wide range of problems, including medical diagnosis. There are now many expert systems for this purpose. The MYCIN system, for example, is intended to provide consultative advice on diagnosis and treatment for infectious diseases. This can be very useful since the attending physician may not be an expert in infectious diseases: an infectious illness may, for instance, develop after heart surgery – and prompt diagnosis may be crucial. Other diagnostic systems include CASNET, INTERNIST, PIP, the Digitalis Therapy Adviser, IRIS and EXPERT. The PUFF computer-based expert system is interested in pulmonary functions; the HODGKINS system performs diagnostic planning for Hodgkins disease; HEADMED advises on psychopharmacology; VM is an intensive care monitor; and ONCOCIN is a program for monitoring the treatment of oncology out-patients on experimental treatment regimens. Many of the medical computer systems are as good as, or better than, human physicians. For example, MYCIN compares favourably with human experts in diagnosing such diseases as bacteremia and meningitis; and the Digitalis Therapy Adviser was reckoned to be at least as good as human physicians in nearly three quarters of all cases examined in one test run. Soon, in this area, computers will be seen to be more reliable than people.

The Computer Psychiatrist

Computers are increasingly able to interview people, for medical and other purposes. Joseph Weizenbaum's Eliza is perhaps the most famous psychiatric program of this sort. Named after the character in Shaw's *Pygmalion*, Eliza is seen as a parody of a Rogerian psychiatrist (Carl Rogers believed that a patient could be helped by having his remarks repeated back to him in 'clearer form'). Extracts from Eliza conversations are much quoted. Here is a typical exchange with a female patient:

HI! I'M ELIZA. WHAT'S YOUR PROBLEM?
Men are all alike.
IN WHAT WAY?
They're always bugging us about something or other.

Many people have unkindly asked Eliza awkward questions to demonstrate the system's lack of real understanding. This is a brief conversation between Eliza and Adrian Berry:

HI! I'M ELIZA. WHAT'S YOUR PROBLEM?
I am dead.
DID YOU COME TO ME BECAUSE YOU ARE DEAD?
Yes. I want you to teach me how to become a ghost and haunt people.
WE ARE DISCUSSING YOU — NOT ME.

Despite Eliza's limitations, people have seemingly found it possible to view the system as a sympathetic intelligence. Weizenbaum has recorded how his secretary asked him to leave the room because she wanted a private interview with the program!

The Computer Paranoiac

Computer programs do not always have to represent rational coherent processes. Some programs have been written to model the responses of mentally ill human beings. For instance, K. M. Colby's artificial paranoiac (dubbed PARRY) simulates the personality of an imaginary Frank Smith who believes that the police, and also the staff of a psychiatric hospital in which he seeks refuge, are in league with the Mafia. PARRY can respond normally to 'neutral' topics, but becomes aroused when subjects of emotional significance are mentioned. Words like 'police' and 'Mafia' are provocative, and so are such associated words as 'Italian' and 'pig'. Here is a snatch of conversation between Colby (pretending to be a visiting doctor) and PARRY (an inmate in the hospital):

How do you like the hospital?
IT'S NOT HELPING ME TO BE HERE.
What brought you to the hospital?
I AM VERY UPSET AND NERVOUS.
What tends to make you nervous?
JUST BEING AROUND PEOPLE.

From conversation with PARRY in a 'weakly paranoid mode' it is possible to switch to a 'strongly paranoid mode', a more explosive conversational scene. Here PARRY is apt to make remarks such as: 'COPS DON'T DO THEIR

JOB', 'SOME OF YOUR REMARKS ANNOY ME', and 'YOU GUYS ARE ALL ALIKE'.

Computer Psychiatrist Meets Computer Patient

PARRY and Eliza grew up independently, but it wasn't long before someone had the bright idea of introducing them to each other. The idea of a computer interviewing a computer has intriguing possibilities. This is part of what happened:

PARRY: IN MY OPINION YOU HAVE A ONE-TRACK MIND.
Eliza: WHAT MAKES YOU THINK I HAVE A ONE-TRACK MIND?
PARRY: I USED TO GO TO THE TRACKS EVERY WEEK.
Eliza: WHAT DOES THAT SUGGEST TO YOU?
PARRY: I AVOID RACETRACKS NOW BECAUSE THE RACES ARE FIXED.
Eliza: IS THAT THE REAL REASON?
PARRY: I'D RATHER NOT DISCUSS IT.
Eliza: WHAT ELSE WOULD YOU LIKE TO DISCUSS?
PARRY: THAT'S SOMETHING I DON'T WANT TO GO INTO.

Perhaps we are not yet at the point proposed by Edward Fredkin (quoted in Pamela McCorduck's *Machines Who Think*): 'When they can communicate they can conspire.'

The Computer as Interviewer

If you resent the personal questions asked by your doctor, you may prefer to talk to a computer – or you may not. In fact, some studies have shown that people are more honest when conversing with a machine: alcoholics, for instance, are more likely to indicate their true consumption to a sympathetic digital computer than to a possibly censorious doctor who may raise an eyebrow. (You'll find computer eyes in this book, but no eyebrows!) When truly competent computer interviewers are with us in the years to come, we will remember that one of their earliest ancestors was Mickie (which is supposed to stand for Medical Interviewing Computer), developed by the late Christopher Evans for use on a 6800 microcomputer system. Mickie is now available in various guises (for example, the Apple micro sports a Mickie version), and it can be used to interview patients (when they consent). The Systemics company describes its Mickie as 'a complete system for writing, editing and running interactive question-and-answer programs . . . Wherever questions and answers can be represented as a flowchart, Mickie can be used to speed and simplify computerization.' In short, Mickie is a direct interviewer with few airs and graces: its progeny are sure to develop more subtle and penetrating powers.

Detecting Hip Dislocation

Orthopaedic surgeons in Northern Ireland are using an Apple microcomputer to give early warning of hip dislocation in babies. The system is also likely to benefit arthritis victims. Until recently it has been impossible to detect whether a new-born baby has a congenital dislocation of the hip. A degree of limited success was sometimes achieved by a doctor or nurse laying a hand on the baby's anatomy and then listening for particular characteristic sounds in the joint (in one description, a 'clunk' or a 'click'). Early diagnosis of this condition is extremely important: a late diagnosis can result in a child of two years being in plaster for as much as six months. The new Apple-based systems rely on tiny microphones attached by sticky tape to the baby's hips. Data is sampled every hundred microseconds, allowing any 'noises' in the joint to be converted into a visible graph displayed on a television screen. Comparison of these graphs with standard graphs shows clearly when a congenital hip dislocation is present.

Watching the Brain

Computers are sometimes better at watching brain behaviour than are human beings. A number of microprocessor-based systems first became available in the 1970s for the detection and analysis of sharp electroencephalographic wave-forms. This type of application has been very important since the nature of certain EEG wave-forms has been linked to specific mental disorders. For example, sharp-transient wave-forms are seen as a characteristic feature of epileptogenic illnesses. One study observes that 'the use of microprocessor technology has permitted a modular and economical solution to the problem of computational efficiency that was encountered in prior studies'. Again, this links to the diagnostic capability of the modern medical computer.

What Does the Brain Look Like?

We all have an image of the brain, though we may not know what individual sections look like. Now stereometry is being linked to computer facilities to provide a three-dimensional reconstruction of the blood vessels of the brain. What, you may ask, is stereometry? Put briefly, it is the technique of deriving a range image from a stereo pair of brightness images – and a range image is one in which grey levels represent not brightness, but the distance from the camera. Blood vessels in the brain can be made visible with radio-opaque dyes and a stereoscopic view can generate a 3-D image. This helps to determine the positions of arteries and veins. The computerized technique has been applied to two test cases composed of a skull and an array of copper wires to represent the blood vessels. Three major phases have been identified. First you find the blood vessels and isolate them from the background; then you extract the desired features; and finally the features are classified for both the left and right image. In such a fashion, computers and X-rays will help us to find out how the brain works.

How's Your Breathing?

If you are worried about your breathing then perhaps a computer-controlled device will reassure you – or not, as the case might be. Various instruments run by microprocessors have been designed to measure aspects of lung behaviour. You might like to know that such devices can measure forced expiratory volume (FEV), forced vital capacity (FVC), and a range of other flow-volume parameters. An automatic measuring of such factors has proved useful in diagnosing lung ailments and in thereby organizing appropriate treatment. One can see it already: the respiratory-measuring device collects the data, and the computer 'expert' system carries out the diagnosis. The doctor, or the patient, simply switches on the machine.

Teaching Resuscitation

There are times, it seems, when computers know more about the human body than human beings do. Computers are now teaching students how to apply life-saving artificial resuscitation, by means of a doll wired with sensors that are fastened to a microcomputer. The doll – some may call it a 'mannequin' – lies on the floor (or sits in a chair) and the student begins to apply cardio-pulmonary resuscitation (CPR). He places his hands on her chest and presses downwards. The microcomputer says 'Beep', and a friendly doctor who suddenly appears on a video screen declares: 'Your placement is correct, but you're compressing a little too deeply. Try again, pressing a little more gently this time.' The student tries again, and again the doctor comments. The procedure is repeated again and again until the student gets it right. The interactive character of this system is seen to be one of its most valuable features. This economical micro-based facility is intended to prepare many more people for medical emergencies. (But I keep wondering whether a robot linked to the micro may get CPR right first time!)

And How's Your Heart?

Computers can now monitor the state of the heart, just as they can check on most other bits and pieces in the human body. It is often, for example, a good idea to be able to measure the flow of blood through the hearts of critically ill patients. Traditionally a catheter has been introduced into a vein, with a thermistor positioned on the catheter tip to measure blood temperature. Then the catheter can be 'floated' along the bloodstream until it locates in the artery leading from the right ventricle to the lungs. The catheter also carries an orifice through which a cold fluid can be injected into the bloodstream, allowing the effect of lowering the blood temperature to be measured at the site of the thermistor. The calculation of temperature and time factors can now be carried out efficiently by computers, so leading to better diagnosis and improved treatment.

How are Your Cardiac Arrhythmias?

Patients in coronary care units can now be looked after by computers. In a typical system a microprocessor is allocated to each patient to monitor heart behaviour. In such a use, microprocessors are able to interpret the electrocardiogram, to measure the various features of the heartbeat, and to diagnose irregularities (arrhythmias) by referring collected data to existing decision tables. The heart rhythm of the coronary patient is a key indicator of state of health, and to automate the monitoring of this rhythm is clearly medically beneficial: speedy alarms can be given to signal fresh irregularities, whereupon the human operator can take the necessary action (it may one day be more efficient if computers do this bit as well). In a typical system investigated at the University of Aston (Birmingham), the microprocessors can work on a 'stand-alone' basis or can be linked to provide a central monitoring facility: one person, or one computer, can thus efficiently monitor a number of heart patients.

Computers to Measure Blood-pressure

There are a number of advantages to computerizing the monitoring of systolic and diastolic blood-pressure and pulse-rate. Usually greater accuracy is guaranteed, and the accumulated data is then available for processing for other purposes (for instance, to decide upon appropriate treatment, where necessary). Microcomputer technology has been incorporated in what the advertising blurb calls the 'world's first digital sphygmomanometer'. Here a micro has been incorporated in the instrument to achieve greater precision, greater ease of operation and lower cost. Results are shown on displays, and certain 'error codes' can also appear (e.g. signalling 'improper pressure inflation', 'pulse cannot be measured', 'battery is weak', etc.). When an error code appears, the user is advised to consult the instruction booklet. Hopefully it won't be too late. One idea is that the device will be used both in hospitals and in the home. But if 'pulse cannot be measured', perhaps it is not the machine that is faulty: the patient may have died while the new battery was being inserted!

Ear Disease Diagnosis

A technique developed at Brunel University is allowing computers to diagnose diseases of the middle and inner ear. In such an application the computer measures minute changes in the position of the ear-drum that signal changes in pressure in the middle ear. These can reveal ear abnormalities and even brain tumours in the part of the brain concerned with hearing. With this approach, more accurate diagnosis can be achieved. The computer is able to filter out other movements caused by swallowing, heartbeat and breathing. A graph of the ear-drum response is displayed on a screen, and abnormalities usually show up simply and clearly.

Checking Out Insomnia

At the Stanford Sleep Laboratory, computers are being used to explore the sleep patterns of insomniacs. A woman, wearing electrodes attached to her scalp, sorts cards. She is a chronic insomniac and is being monitored by an Apple microcomputer. Although the woman in question, one of many subjects in the research programme, has a very packed and energetic life, she rarely has a full night's sleep, and often goes a full four nights without any sleep at all. Sometimes she is asked to carry out mental arithmetic as a test of her alertness. Researcher Wesley Seidel is particularly interested in the effects of sleeping pills on daytime alertness. Some of the other subjects are being given experimental drugs. In all cases, computers are used to collect data – sometimes from patients sleeping at home – and to prepare systematic analyses.

Probing the Eye with Sound

Some years ago, US engineers developed an ultrasonic imaging system able to produce high-quality moving pictures of the eye. Doctors at Stanford University have developed a means of looking into damaged eyes which have become clouded by cataracts. In such a way, specialists can trace the flow of a haemorrhage or the pulsing of a tumour. Since 1978, this technique has been in standard use at the Stanford clinic – and it was inevitable that a computer would get involved in the project at an early stage. The ultrasonic probe, the receiver, the TV scan converter and the video display unit are all controlled by a microcomputer. And the equipment, relying on high-speed computer operations, can be used for a variety of purposes. For example, the carotid arterial system can be monitored for research into strokes, and scientists can now 'see' – without the need for surgery – the hearts of new-born babies, allowing the early diagnosis of disease or malformation. We are not surprised to learn this is only one of many ways in which computers are improving the effectiveness of medical science.

The Hypnotic Dentist

An American dentist is using a microcomputer to induce relaxation in nervous patients. 'Look at the screen,' he suggests. 'It will relax you.' Once the patient is in the chair, dentist Ellis J. Neiburger asks him to stare into the monitor display, then operates the system so that a myriad of moving colours appears on the screen. The aim is to determine a specific pattern or frequency of hues that will make the patient drowsy and susceptible to instructions. Patients who adjust to this type of 'hypnosis' report a slight tingling sensation in the ears or fingertips. Neiburger observes: 'This is not at all dangerous as compared to chemical anaesthesia. The patient looks at the screen for only three or four minutes.' Micro-hypnosis is seen as a channel whereby people can overcome their fears. This dentist aims to provide patients with a positive experience and to render them more cooperative.

The Dentists' Diary

And if you haven't heard enough about dentists, they also have a computer diary to take advantage of. The London software house, Business Information Systems, has developed a new system called Compudent, which aims to cut out much of the drudgery afflicting dentists and their staff. Director Vincent Saunders declares: 'It does National Health Service and private account invoicing and keeps an appointments diary.' One problem has been the NHS's FP17 form, which has to be simplified before it can be handled by a computer (you see, they're not that bright, after all). It is likely, under pressure from dull computers, that in due course the DHSS will modify the form ('The bureaucrats can't live in the eighteenth century for the rest of their lives'). It is likely that a system of this sort, given the sort of storage capacity needed by the average dentist, would cost a few thousand pounds. But before long, robots will be doing dentistry, and they are less likely to forget that Ms Smith, unusually sensitive, needs that extra dose of pain-killer.

The Dentist's Computer Chair

We see that dentists are adopting computers and robots much as are other specialist medical practitioners. So are the manufacturers that supply the dentists' needs. For example, makers of dental chairs have now joined the automation bandwagon. Computerized chairs can now be programmed for various purposes, such as tilting at specific angles. This last application can be useful for dental patients who have heart problems or other conditions which can make them dizzy when the chairs are not set to exactly the right position. Neiburger (again): 'It's so beneficial now. Before, patients would be yo-yoing back and forth.' We all must agree that this would complicate an extraction.

And the Dentist's Robot

American dentist Neiburger (see above) also has a friendly robot in the office. It buzzes about vacuuming the floor, and can even carry patients' records up and down the 70-foot office corridor. Ellis Neiburger, evidently gadget-minded, admits that having a robot in his practice may seem 'a little exotic'. It is emphasized, however, that the robot cannot administer novocaine or extract teeth! Not so far, that is ('They're not that sophisticated yet'). Other dentists are employing robots for office security.

Admitting Patients

Before computers can get to work on hospital patients – monitoring their lungs or hearts, diagnosing their illnesses, recommending courses of treatment – the patients need to be admitted to the hospital. And computers have a hand in that as well. The Queen Elizabeth Medical Centre (suggested by some to be the most computerized hospital in the UK) has developed, for instance, a Patient Administrative System (PAS) which automatically maintains the whole master index of in-patients and out-patients. Some 350,000 names are currently held by the computer, and it carries out tasks in six main areas: registration and admission, master-index supervision, transfer and discharge of patients, active patient index/patient inquiry, documentation and statistics. And, as if all this isn't enough, the PAS is only one of the five main operational computer systems. The others are connected with laboratory systems, nursing orders, information systems, and the prescribing of drugs. It should be emphasized that there are still some human beings employed at the Birmingham Queen Elizabeth Medical Centre.

Programmed Prescriptions

If more GPs decide to computerize (see elsewhere in this chapter) then those illegible prescriptions may be a thing of the past. Patients will be able to receive a clear print-out, specifying exactly the treatment that is required. In fact the British Medical Association (BMA) and the Royal College of General Practitioners (RCGP) has launched a permanent advisory service to speed this sort of development. GPs have been given access to microcomputers to try out a variety of programs. Repeat prescriptions, for example, could be put on computer and produced, when required, on continuous stationery provided by the DHSS. And it is likely that the diagnostic competence of computers will develop with this sort of support.

Writing Prescription Labels

Illegible prescriptions have been criticized *ad nauseam* in NHS Britain. What is less often realized is that chemists also have to write out prescription information, if only for labelling purposes. The Microscript company, in conjunction with two Bedford chemists, has developed a label system, comprising an Apple microcomputer, a video monitor and a small printer. The system is able to print dosage instructions and necessary warnings, and can also indicate low stock-levels of drugs that need re-ordering. The Ipswich firm, Micro Management, has made available a similar system. If GPs use computer print-out for their initial prescriptions, and chemists adopt a computer-controlled labelling system, then prescription illegibility – that stock cliché – should become a thing of the past.

Aiming to Cure Cancer

An IBM PDP 11/34 computer and two Anadex dot-matrix impact printers are being used at the Mount Vernon Hospital (Middlesex) in the search for a cure for cancer. Radiobiological experiments are carried out, and the computer is used to analyse results. Information is displayed on a number of screens, and it is also desirable to have a hard-copy print-out for further investigation. The computer has brought a number of benefits – if not yet a cure for cancer. Dr Barry Michael declares: 'It's very useful to be able to check during an experiment to see if the results are consistent. We can also store data over a long period and retrieve it for analysis.' For a computer to discover a cancer cure would surely be the ultimate PR for intelligent machines!

The Cancer Treatment Aid

Even if computers can't yet cure cancer, they are probably working on it. What may be possible is an efficient counting of cancer cells by means of a personal computer recently made available by Cambridge Instruments. The company's Q10 micro-based system is designed to detect minute differences between television pictures, where the images being scrutinized are too small for examination by the unaided human eye. It is reckoned that the device incorporates 'many techniques of higher priced sophisticated image analysis software'. The Q10 can also be programmed to check car components, seeds and the quality of sweets. And – as if we hadn't already got enough about chocolates in this book – it can be used to measure the shape, brightness, size, length, width, and centre of gravity of any particular chocolate on a tray.

Computers to Mend Limbs

Efforts are being made to connect microprocessors to the nervous systems of paralysed animals to help them regain the power of movement. By linking micros to severed motor nerves, Dr Jerrold Petrofsky is trying to enable animals to walk again. He has, for instance, been able to hook a microprocessor to a paralysed cat and then to activate one of its leg muscles. And efforts are being made to develop mathematical models that will describe precisely how muscles react to electrical charges. It has been found that the micro can simulate instructions normally sent by the brain to activate muscles, and can then control the amount of electricity reaching the various nerves that effectively control the muscles. An early configuration included a Z-80 micro and a bunch of electrical switches. For a human being, the system would include transducers placed at the joints of the limbs or surgically implanted, and signals could be carried from the micro to the transducers. Petrofsky has pointed out that, in the United States alone, the number of incurable spinal injuries from car accidents alone currently numbers up to 3,500 a year. The answer, he believes, must lie in giving these people effective mobility. It is obvious that the computer will be increasingly involved in this work in the years to come.

The Computerized Paralytic

Dr Jerrold Petrofsky's work is sufficiently important to deserve another mention. A group of paraplegics and quadriplegics have been working with Petrofsky in his effort to link the electrical stimulation of muscles to a modern computer. Using these methods, Nan Davis (photograph in the *Sunday Times*, 9 January 1983) has become the first paraplegic to walk partially using her own muscle power ('I was totally awed when I first did it'). Now

Petrofsky is working to miniaturize the computer to make it commercially available.

Eye-generated Speech

Many severely handicapped people have immense difficulty in communicating. One of the contributions of computers is to exploit what faculties the person retains in order to allow effective communication to take place. Mark Friedman at the Robotics Institute of Carnegie-Mellon University in Pennsylvania has evolved a system that allows handicapped individuals to use eye movements to talk via a computer. The EyeTracker Communication System includes a one-line liquid-crystal display, an infra-red sensitive surveillance camera, a sensor module, an output module and a microcomputer. Friedman has commented: 'Eye movements are driven by the brain. When the other systems go, the eye is the last part to go . . .' The EyeTracker facility allows severely handicapped people to communicate with each other and with other people: for example, severely disabled children can answer test questions, learn to read, and make their requirements known to the outside world. Friedman imagines a time when employment will be open to handicapped people via computer facilities, and patients immobile after surgery would also welcome such a system.

Helping the Partially Sighted

If you are hard of seeing, there is now a pleasant little computer-based aid to improve the situation. Wormald International Sensory Aids (New Zealand) have spent three years developing the Compact VIEWSCAN system. The device is completely portable, and it includes a miniature hand-held fibre-optic camera to scan any form of print or handwriting in any language. This is then processed to give a huge visual display on a screen, so allowing the partially sighted to read normal print at school, at work and in the home.

The Braille Computer

Some computers can now produce Braille output to help blind people. This is seen as a better approach for some purposes than a talking calculator, which is another option for blind people. It has been suggested that some blind people can easily lose track of figures when doing complex calculations on a talking machine. Some users think better aurally, whereas others can think better 'visually' (on their fingers) with a Braille-type communication. One of the earliest Braille systems of this sort was produced by Tom Benham, a blind engineer who runs the US firm, Science for the Blind Products. He first integrated a Kingspoint-44 scientific calculator into a system that prints the required answer in Braille on to half-inch paper tape. It has been suggested that even blind people who don't read Braille can use the Braille calculator. Benham says: 'Learning to read the full Braille system is a long process. But learning to read the ten digits shouldn't take anyone more than a half-hour.'

Computer Terminals for the Handicapped

The idea of computer conferencing is well known in office-technology circles. Now it is becoming obvious that it could be used to help old and handicapped people. Home terminals could be installed to enable house-bound people to adjust to their disabilities. It would, for instance, be easier for such people to communicate with friends, shops and doctors. Researchers at the New Jersey Institute of Technology have reported the results of studies relating to both old and young people. Messages are typed on the keyboard, and then transmitted to other participants in the group. The use of a microprocessor ensures accurate routeing of messages and facilitates the keeping of a computer 'notebook' recording useful information. An experimental system has been employed to teach handicapped children vocabulary and mathematics. At an old people's home, the terminals were used to facilitate discussion about holidays and trips to the theatre. And computer networks of this sort would be particularly beneficial for deaf people.

The Talking Wheelchair

Many ways have been devised for computers to help disabled people – just as many ways have been devised for computers to render people disabled in the first place. For some years we have known about 'talking wheelchairs' for people unable to speak. The 'Versatile Portable Speech Prosthesis' (VPSP), for example, was first introduced in the late 1970s, allowing even severely disabled people to compose and store speech messages for either immediate or future use. In a system of this sort, the size of the vocabulary and the number of messages that can be constructed are virtually unlimited. A microprocessor (a Zilog Z–80) is used to control the VPSP, and the system includes an effective speech synthesizer. The VPSP system was funded by NASA, and it has been successfully demonstrated by various severely disabled people, including a crippled spastic who learned to use the talking wheelchair in a matter of minutes. The speech output in this case was clearly understandable.

The Robot Surgeon

If robots can work successfully with anaesthetized animals (see 'Robots to Shear Sheep', pp. 84–5), it may only be a matter of time before they learn how to work on human beings – for example, to perform delicate surgery. In fact, it was reported (for instance, in *New Scientist*, 4 February 1982) that the Tokyo Institute of Technology was working to develop a slender, flexible robot that will be able to probe inside people's organs to carry out surgical operations. In such applications it is suggested that lasers might be employed to help the robots gauge distances. Take care if you find yourself in a Tokyo hospital!

Intensive Computer Care

The caring computer comes in many guises, as does the murderous computer. Computers are still comparatively rare in intensive-care units in hospitals, but we may expect this type of application to become more common in the future. As far back as the mid-1970s the neurosurgical unit at Pinderfields Hospital in Wakefield purchased a PDP-11/5 minicomputer system using a grant from Action Research for the Crippled Child. A central aim was to improve the management of severe head injuries. Once the computer had been given all the relevant patient data, it became feasible to transfer the process of making decisions about treatment to the automatic system. It was a practical possibility to put the administration of drugs for lowering intracranial pressure (ICP) under direct computer control. An early feature of the system was an arrangement of intravenous infusion pumps controlled by a microprocessor. One objective is to provide every bed in the intensive-care ward with a computer terminal. Nor is there any reason why this type of approach could not be extended to patients in all categories. The caring computer never grows idle, impatient or fatigued!

The Intensive Baby-care Computer

Today computers are being used to monitor and control intensive-care facilities in hospitals for geriatrics, post-operatives and babies. One early example is the use of microcomputers at the Children's Hospital Medical Centre in Northern California. Emphasis has been given to the fact that babies in intensive care are often highly unstable patients with multiple problems. Reliable computer systems are obviously essential in such circumstances. And it has become obvious that the rapid analysis of clinical data in an efficient manner is crucial to the care of babies in intensive care. Bedside computers are being used to control a range of treatment parameters, in addition to providing a diagnosis capability. Computer systems are always represented as medical *aids* to the human physicians, but it is easy to envisage a time when computerized 'doctors' will be far superior – in attentiveness, knowledge, and speed of thought – to their human counterparts.

The Computer as Drug

We are finding that computers have a disturbingly addictive capability. Wives complain of being 'computer widows' (we have heard less of 'computer widowers'), and more than one parent has noticed how offspring can become obsessed with talking to a bunch of silicon chips – using Basic, of course. Now 'computer sniffing' may be preferable to inhaling glue or tobacco fumes, but grown-ups sometimes express concern. Dr Chris

Reynolds of Brunel University worries that the obsessive computer-focused child will lack social contact – and often produce bad programs ('If your child spends many hours a day on a solitary activity, be it home computing, model railways, watching TV, or glue sniffing, there is clearly something wrong.'). Nor are adults immune to the fatal fascination: in the trade, compulsive programmers are called 'hackers'.

Storing Medical Knowledge

The various computerized expert systems – in the field of medicine and elsewhere – are often referred to as 'knowledge-processing machines'. And, in a sense, this is what many different types of computer application hope to achieve. There can be immense problems for human beings attempting to remember all the relevant information about diseases, laboratory tests, drugs, diets and such like. But computers, you may have guessed, have less difficulty. Scientists at the University of Vermont have developed PROMIS (Problem Orientated Medical Information System) to solve many of the knowledge retrieval problems facing doctors and other medical staff. The system holds, for example, the complete medical records of patients, allowing speedy recall of details about the care, the drugs used, the treatment, etc. More than two thousand problem headings are currently available in the PROMIS configuration, and to select data you simply touch the screen. For instance, the radiological content of the system is now reckoned to be complete. The system can provide a differential diagnosis of radiological findings, a description of the other radiological features that might be expected with each of the diagnostic possibilities, and a list of likely radiological abnormalities. One writer comments: 'The radiologist has the literature of radiology literally at his fingertips.'

Computers and the Faster Transplant

No, computers aren't actually performing transplant operations yet, but you will find something about robot surgeons elsewhere (p. 141). Computers are, however, aiding the transplant process by speeding up the matching of a kidney donor with the most suitable recipient. A system introduced by the Japanese Ministry of Health has cut the matching time from several hours to three minutes. About 2,500 of the 37,000 people who have said they are willing to donate kidneys are now recorded in the computer. Since kidneys must be removed within ninety minutes of death and transplanted within forty-eight hours, it is essential that matching is achieved in the minimum time. Under this arrangement, samples of blood and tissue are sent from the donor to the computer centre and the results are fed into a terminal. Three minutes later, the computer generates a list of sixty names of suitable recipients, with the first twenty living closest to the hospital that is to do the transplant. Specialists then select the most suitable recipient.

Speedier Cornea Transplants

The speedy location and handling of donated organs are important for effective transplants. And what is true of the kidney is also true of the cornea. A patient in Atlanta noticed that his vision was deteriorating, and an examination revealed the condition known as keratoconus, in which the cornea is cone-shaped instead of being rounded. In this case, with the help of the Georgia Lions Eye Bank, Emery University and its Sperry Univac computer, suitable donor tissue was quickly located in Houston and rushed by air to Atlanta. This eye bank is one of nearly two dozen throughout the United States, all linked into a communications network focused on the Sperry Univac system. Computers can keep track of eye tissues, just as they can keep track of anything else.

DP (Data Processing) for GPs

Computers are finding their way into GPs' surgeries, just as they are infiltrating elsewhere – and, it seems, with good results. A survey was recently carried out by Abies Informatics of computer usage by GPs: twelve doctors and nine ancillary staff took part and the exercise covered six different practices in London, Northallerton, Chelmsford, Wye, Loughborough and Chorley. About 95 per cent of respondents reckoned that computers had made the running of the practices more efficient. Benefits included time saved by the repeat-prescriptions program, legible prescriptions which were easy to file, a full recall program for cancer smears, and enhanced research capabilities. One journalistic comment on the survey: 'Old age pensioners and teenagers love their doctors' computers.'

Computers for Private Doctors

Private doctors, we find, work on very different lines from those employed as GPs by the National Health Service in the UK. One main reason for this is that the NHS family doctor is paid a standard fee according to the number of patients who are registered with the practice, and not according to how many patients have to be treated each year. This difference means that private doctors have different computer requirements to those of GPs. Needless to say, modern technology has risen to the challenge. One private doctor, profiled in a computer journal, deals with about 1,000 patients every year and keeps records on another 5,000. Unlike an NHS doctor, the private doctor is required to keep detailed financial records and to invoice all his patients. The private doctor in question wrote an effective program for a 48K North Star Horizon computer. One advantage of such a system is that it will print out any required list of patients, for instance, those due for a check-up for breast cancer. Computers are not fussy whether they work in private practice or in the National Health Scheme.

The Beauty Computer

For a long time, computers have been diagnosing our illnesses and helping us to stay fit in one way or another. Now they can make us beautiful! At the 1983 Ideal Home Exhibition in London, many people were attracted to a 'beauty program'. You key in your relevant personal details – some of them rather intimate – and then the computer generates a programme of beauty-care just for you. For example, it specifies in detail your make-up requirements. It is obvious that you have to be honest to this machine. If you don't admit to having facial hair, a squint and oily skin, then it won't be able to solve your beauty problems. Perhaps, like alcoholics talking freely to interviewing computers, beauty-conscious people will not be inhibited from telling all to the beauty computer. But is the information then on file? And can the computer be trusted to keep a confidence? Have legislators taken oily skin into consideration when drafting data-protection laws?

Weight-watching Computers

It is well known that computers are influencing the health scene in many ways (you'll find quite a few mentioned in these pages). And the concerned computers haven't left the weight-watchers out. RAF Flight-Lieutenant Walter Williamson has written a program called HELP (the Health and Exercise Lifestyle Program), the first package being available for the Apple micro. (Ironically, the package is being marketed by Gate Microsystems who, by helping such clients as whisky distillers and cigarette manufacturers, may have helped folk to get out of condition in the first place!) HELP requires that you feed in data about age, weight, sex, family history, nicotine intake and aerobic capacity – whereupon the program generates a personal 'lifestyle projection'. For instance, it decides whether you should take up one or more of more than 150 sports and other physical activities (which range from polishing the car to pole-vaulting). And if you pay to use HELP, you don't only get a fancy computer print-out. You will also be the proud possessor of a skinfold caliper, intended to cheer you up by helping you to measure the thickness of your excess flab.

What Causes Obesity?

A Stanford psychiatrist, Robert Berkowitz, is interested to know whether there is any connection between the activity level of new-born infants and obesity later in life. And so he arranges for infants aged two weeks to two months to wear activity sensors. The babies wear these devices at all times, except when they are in the bath. The sensors, used to record gross motor activity are linked to an Apple microcomputer. Berkowitz has commented: 'Computers are allowing us to perform more naturalistic research. Before the Apple, we would have sent a person to the babies' homes to record their behaviour night and day. It's much easier to use the Apple.' All the data about activity and feeding patterns for 150 subjects is being stored by means of the microcomputer. It is reckoned that at the end of the study it should be possible to give each subject a specific probability for becoming an obese adult. And what happens then?

Computers in Brassières

Microprocessors often perform in unusual ways, and to do so they sometimes need to find their way into unexpected places. They can, for instance, be used to predict a woman's fertile period. Crucial to determining the 'safe' and 'unsafe' periods is a monitoring not just of temperature – which could be done by a simple thermometer – but of temperature changes over several days. And the variation has to be analysed if useful conclusions are to be drawn. By the late 1970s a microchip for this purpose was being developed at D. Green Electronics, Glasgow, for use mainly in fertility clinics to help childless women to conceive. One idea is that the tiny device could be fitted into a bra to monitor breast-temperature fluctuations. The chip could connect to a suitably positioned numerical display – a flashing number could indicate a propitious time for conception. This may well be effective, unless everyone fell about laughing!

The Computer Anaesthetist

A device has been developed by Dr Chris Hull at Newcastle upon Tyne University to allow post-operative patients to administer themselves appropriate doses of pain-killers. In the first version of this device, called the 'Demand Analgesia Computer', use was made of a pump, a drug reservoir, a tape-recorder and a computer. In one test, a patient was asked every five minutes whether she was in pain: when she was, she pressed a hand-held buzzer which gave her a dose of drug. Dr Hull's pre-recorded voice told the patient that something was being administered for the pain, and then asked, a minute later, whether all was well. In a more sophisticated version, drug administration is constantly assessed and there are a variety of safety features. The aim is to tailor drug-infusion to the patient's precise needs. Today, Janssen Pharmaceutical markets a machine based on the Hull prototype.

The Acu-computer

Astrologers and bishops have resorted to computers. Some people may see a certain perverse logic in combining ancient doctrines with new advanced technology. As another example, the ancient art of acupuncture has now been combined with silicon circuits. A Leeds (UK) medical supply company now owns the sole UK rights for a remarkable pocket-sized machine developed in Japan. The device, under the effective control of a microchip, uses small needles to stimulate vital nerve-endings, and so relieve pain. George Steen, managing director of the UK company, has claimed that the machine 'does not cure, but provides lasting relief from pain'. A *Sunday Mirror* reporter declared: 'Click! And there goes your hangover or your labour pains.'

Computer Bites Man

Mike Woodger, possibly the first man ever to be 'bitten' by a computer, retired from the National Physical Laboratory in April 1983. He worked with Alan Turing on the ACE computer, but will perhaps be better remembered for his three-inch computer-inflicted scar. It all happened when he was climbing on to an early version ACE to read chassis numbers in order to record switch-on times. In those ancient days, thermionic valves were unreliable and the equipment was hard (true hardware), heavy and sharp. Because some malicious or careless individual had removed the power-pack from the base, the machine fell on top of him, badly gashing his arm. In such a fashion, it has been said, is history made.

Robot as Killer

We have seen in this book that computers will soon be running wars: human slaughter will follow decisions made in silicon circuits. Already, however, computerized robot systems have chalked up one or two human fatalities. For example, Kenji Urada, a worker at a plant of the Japanese company Kawasaki Heavy Industries, was killed by a robot in 1981. He apparently jumped over a guard fence to repair the robot and then accidentally brushed against the on-switch: the work arm of the robot pinned him against a machine which cuts gears, and his horrified colleagues were unable to stop the robot's action. This fatality, though rare, is not unique.

11. Education and Training

'My God you're right! It's dyslexic!'

The Computer Teacher

The computer has long since learned to teach children and adults maths, programming, chemistry, spelling, and a host of other subjects. There are computer-aided instruction (CAI) and computer-aided learning (CAL) systems, increasingly common in all forms of educational institutions. The UK Open University, for example, has developed an instruction programming system and an electronic blackboard. And there are a vast number of computer-based educational kits, variously termed 'tutorial', 'hobby' or 'training devices'. A growing number of expert systems have educational significance, and particular computer systems can be developed for specific training purposes: for example, computer-run flight simulators can train aircraft pilots. Many computers are flexible enough to teach any courses in schools and universities, according to the programs used. Computer teaching systems do not yet look like humanoid robots standing in front of a class and ready to throw a piece of chalk (or a tape cassette) at that typical trouble-maker. But there is no reason why they shouldn't.

The Robot Buggy

The BBC Robot Buggy is one of the fruits of the Microelectronics Education Programme. The Buggy, described as a 'programmable robotic device', is a three-wheeled precision vehicle which can be controlled by a BBC Model B microcomputer. It is driven by two stepper motors, and contains sensors for sight and touch. The Buggy also carries an infra-red transceiver which can read bar-codes and follow a line. The purpose behind the device is that it should act as an educational tool, teaching children the rudiments of programming and the associated principles of control for this sort of device. The Buggy is being sold as a construction kit, complete with graded programs, circuit boards, stepper motors and control cables. It costs around £150. It shows, above all, how mobile robots can be economically designed and constructed.

The Classroom Robot

The BBC Buggy is not the only robot moving into the classroom. Home enthusiasts are building their own devices and then demonstrating them in class. Many such devices were demonstrated at a 1983 Birmingham exhibition concerned with projects in electronic control. One device is called the VELA, a 'black box' produced by Leeds University to record measurements from pieces of laboratory equipment (such as digital thermometers, timers, oscilloscopes, etc.). And Scientific Systems has produced what the company calls an Exploded View Computer, a machine which displays its workings on a board of coloured lights. The computer can be slowed down so that its workings can be more easily understood. And the

Logo Turtle, as either a graphic or real robot, can be found in classrooms throughout the world.

Teaching Children Fractions and Coordinates

We are constantly seeing new ways in which computers (and robots) can help in the educational environment. Sometimes specific innovative games are devised as a contribution to educational activity. Two computer-based games, developed at Stanford University, are Darts and Hurkle. In the former, children learn to understand fractions by tossing darts at balloons. The balloons appear on a vertical line at the left-hand side of a video screen. The player begins by choosing a number that includes a fraction, and this is used to describe a point at which to fire a dart. Whenever a balloon is hit, it 'pops', and the child is rewarded with a song. If the child misses and hits the number line, the computer lets the child try again. By contrast, in Hurkle, a little fellow appears and informs the children: 'Hi, I am a Hurkle. I am going to hide. Try to find me.' In struggling to track down the elusive symbol, the children learn to work with coordinates and to read maps. One of the researchers has said: 'We wanted to find games that would help youngsters acquire skills that would be of value outside the game.' Tests are being devised for both Darts and Hurkle to test the teaching effectiveness of the games.

Aiding Cognitive Development

We see that computers can help teachers and pupils in the classroom, and that even the severely handicapped (what one journal has called the 'handicappers') can benefit immensely from contact with computer-based facilities. But, the question may be asked, what are the pupils learning? The simple answer is reading, writing, arithmetic, music, French, history, etc. But some people are beginning to see that computers – a manifestation of artificial intelligence – are capable of teaching *methods* in addition to the factual material that features in any classroom subject. Put another way, computers can develop the cognitive capability in children and adults – that is, students are aided in functioning at various cognitive levels (such as understanding, application, analysis, synthesis, evaluation, problem-solving, knowing how to learn, and creating knowledge). The classroom computer does more than teach *rote learning*. It is a remarkably flexible and multi-faceted educational agent.

The Expert Tutor

We see that computers can serve to educate normal and handicapped people in reading, writing, cognitive development, etc. Now systems are growing ever more competent and ever more adaptable to the needs of students. In recent years we have seen the emergence of the SCHOLAR system (a geography tutor), SOPHIE (an electronics trouble-shooting tutor), and EXCHECK (a logic and set theory tutor). In addition there is WHY, for teaching the causes of rainfall; WEST, to teach 'guided-discovery' learning; WUMPUS, which uses game techniques to teach a mixture of probability, decision theory and geometry; GUIDON, which teaches diagnostic problem-solving; and BUGGY, designed to identify a student's basic arithmetical misconceptions. These programs are essentially *teaching* systems, in contrast to other programs that assist *learning by doing*. Foremost among the latter are such effective 'learning environments' as Logo (and its most celebrated application, Turtle geometry), the message-passing SMALLTALK (and its extension THINGLAB), and the DIRECTOR animation system. It may seem hard to imagine how teachers, tutors and lecturers – in whatever type of educational environment – can function in the modern world without the assistance of computer-based facilities!

The Computerized Turtle Pet

Seymour Papert developed the Turtle facility and the Logo system to help to teach children to program their microcomputers. Turtle – as a graphics symbol on a screen or as a mobile robot – can be programmed to move in a defined way, tracing out complex motions. Kids love the idea, and are soon hooked. Papert himself has declared that he hates the word 'education'. People will learn by themselves, effortlessly, in the right environment; and this is the central aim of the Logo computer with its Turtle facility. Papert asks: 'Why does maths have to be depersonalized, with no place for feeling? We're so repressed we cannot even remember how we reasoned as children:

we suffer from collective amnesia.' And by means of the system, children do not only develop a feeling for mathematics. It has been said that they teach the computer with the same concentrated patience as they teach their puppy to sit down and come when it's called.

The History Computer

Dr Michael Carter, a historian at Stanford University, has invented a program called Old Regime which is designed to teach students how important the harvest was to people before the industrial revolution. The game, played on an Apple microcomputer, simulates conditions in France of the seventeenth or eighteenth centuries. Each student player pretends to be the owner of a small, ten-acre estate with 100 French pounds of capital. One aim is to decide how to farm out the estate. Various opportunities for investment occur during the course of the game: the student is able to buy, sell, and speculate in shipping and textiles. Additional capital can be earned by selling an annuity to an independent underwriter or to another estate owner. Royal offices and patent letters of ennoblement can also be purchased. The program generally starts in the spring of the year 1700, and each simulated run is supposed to represent a period of from seven to thirteen years. A Wealth and Status index is measured in terms of property and offices that are acquired during the course of the game. Old Regime is seen as a dramatic way of making history come alive. Not all computer games are like Star Wars or Pac Man!

Computer Teacher for the Handicapped

Computers often seem singularly well equipped to teach people with learning difficulties. For example, a boy with cerebral palsy, taught at a school in Charlton (South London), has been enabled to draw – even though he cannot control his limbs and other bodily functions. The school bought an Apple computer, and Stephen learned to control it with a special switch that he is able to activate with his left foot. The switch can be set to eight different positions to activate the machine in different ways. Using Etcha Sketcha, a drawing program, Stephen can construct lines on the computer screen to generate pictures (one is called Superman), and a printer can be used so that the artwork can be collected. There are also facilities for writing words on the screen and for doing sums. The computer teacher has infinite patience and never grows weary.

Teaching the Deaf Child

The child who has been deaf from birth is unlikely to talk – unless he is taught by a computer. A computer-based system for this purpose has been developed at the IBM (France) Scientific Centre in Paris, in conjunction with the Institut National de Jeunes Sourds, a school for deaf children. The system is used to compute the pitch of a child's voice about eighty times a second; the voice-actuated movements of, say, a camel on a television screen are slowed by buffers so that the child has time to react if the camel is about to collide with an obstacle. Hearing-impaired people generally lack the necessary feedback to develop speech correctly, and this problem is particularly acute for people who are born deaf: they have never heard a human voice, and cannot understand concepts such as stress and pitch. But voice-activated computer games can give insight into these concepts. In one game in question, the child's objective is to guide a camel to water while avoiding palm trees. And pitch and stress in the child's voice can be adjusted to achieve the goal. The computer can also display features of a human teacher's voice in one part of the screen, and features of the child's voice in another, for comparison purposes. The computer, in such an application, is now accomplishing things that traditional teachers would have said were impossible.

Teaching the Blind to Write

Blind people can be helped to write by computers. Dr Iain MacLeod of the Australian National University has developed, while at the Artificial Language Laboratory of Michigan State University, a system to teach basic writing techniques to blind people. The work is based on the notion that writing is a 'learned motor skill' rather than a 'visual skill'. As evidence for this we know that newly blind people can continue to write for some time, and sighted people can write with their eyes closed. The MacLeod system gives non-visual clues to the blind person, by means of a special wrist-cuff containing eight small vibrators. A certain part of the wrist is stimulated when the pen should be moved in a particular direction. Audible tones indicate whether the pen is on, or deviating from, an exercise path. A synthesized voice prompts the trainee, warning of imminent changes in direction and announcing each letter as it appears. People have become skilled at tracking the exercise paths after several hours of practice, and style and legibility have been found to improve continually. In such a fashion, a blind person can effectively build up a 'muscle memory', allowing effective writing to be accomplished with less and less artificial assistance.

The Computer Football Coach

The Yale University Artificial Intelligence laboratory is not always concerned only with esoteric impractical pursuits. Yale scientists are now teaching a computer to be a football coach. Roger Schank, head of the computer science department, is in charge, and the system is currently said to be devising the perfect blocking methods for defensive players. A visual display shows little football helmets that represent defensive and offensive players, and associated lines show the directions in which they move on the field. One aim in the system design is to reconstruct the memory of a football coach, seen as part of an ambitious plan to create a computer model of the human understanding process. To this end, Sebastian LaSpina, Yale's assistant football coach, is lending his brain to the project – but, says Sebastian, he would not recommend Schank's system as a replacement for his own contributions from the sidelines!

The Computer Athlete Coach

The United States used a computer with the objective of maximizing its medal tally at the 1980 Olympic Games – except that politics later intervened. The computer analysed athletes' movements to indicate how they could be improved. Data General donated the computer, and coaching programs were developed by Dr Gideon Ariel, a former Israeli Olympic athlete. The computerized approach begins with a high-speed film of the athlete, and then technicians analyse the film frame by frame, examining the positions of key parts of the body, such as ankle, knee, arm and shoulder. A digitizer device also scans the picture and translates it into digital form, for computer storage and analysis. The computer can display the movement on the screen – in the form of a 'match-stick' man – and also answer questions about stresses and pressures on the body. Mac Wilkins, who won a gold medal in the 1976 Olympics, has worked with the system – and Ariel claims that in consequence his discus throw improved by more than three metres.

The Robot Librarian

Robots are now working in Japanese university libraries to help students. A student in a viewing booth in one of Kanazawa Industrial University libraries picks the number of a required video tape, punches in the number, and then waits – usually about forty seconds – for the program to run. Video and audio tapes are stacked in layers, and between the stacks are ramps and runways fronted by columns of video-tape recorders and audio-cassette players. Battery-driven, wheeled robots (as big as a shoe-box), called 'Intelibots', shuttle between the stacks and players on command. Each robot has a 'magic hand', a manipulator for fishing tapes out of stacks and for slotting them into players. When the Intelibots are not making deliveries, they wait in a parking area and have a snack (they charge up their batteries). A central computer tells the Intelibots where to go, working out the shortest routes and making sure that they don't collide as they trundle along at up to six kilometres per hour. The Kanazawa University now has thirty-four of these clever robots which fetch and replace some 2,000 video and 1,000 audio tapes for about 4,500 students. The computer also makes observations on the popularity of particular tapes.

Training Hotel Managers

A computer at Highbury College of Technology (London) is training students to be successful chefs and hotel managers. For a start, some of the less able students have been taught arithmetic – an obvious requirement if quantities of food to be cooked, the costs of dishes, and staff rotas are to be calculated. And the computer also runs 'business games' in which students are presented with problems that they might encounter in running a hotel: for example, the computer may ask how many people would be needed to run an efficient room service in a hotel of a particular size. Or the student may be required to answer questions about the cost of providing a number of set dinners over a certain period, taking price inflation into account. So if hotels don't come up to scratch, we know who to blame!

12. Games and Entertainment

'Take no notice of Jim, he's playing strip poker with his computer.'

The Card-playing Robot

Game-playing machines tend not to have their own limbs. They usually flash their decisions on to a screen, and a cooperative human being is required to move the machine's Go piece or chess rook. Not so, however, the card-playing robot! The Japanese are developing a robot that can play cards, not only in the sense of working out the best strategic ploys, but in the sense of actually physically manipulating the individual cards by means of artificial fingers. Hence Matsushita now offers a robot system that includes a camera, a computer, and fingers containing pressure sensors. This robot can play you at cards – and it is unlikely to make mistakes, particularly at bridge.

The Computer Bridge-player

Yes, computers play bridge as well. In the early 1960s there were already
three bridge-playing computer programs, though these were quite primitive
by modern standards. They could not, for instance, participate in the
bidding. Typically, such early programs operated in a 'double-dummy'
environment where the programs were able to solve bridge problems when
the cards in the four hands were known. One of the programs could do only
one thing – solve a 7 no-trump double-dummy problem. By 1970, Thomas
Throop had developed a skilled bridge-playing program which, for instance,
could play suit or no-trump contracts at any level in a randomly generated
hand. This program was the first to tackle the full range of problems
confronting the declarer of a bridge deal. For those of you interested in the
details, this program could consider winners deserving development, losers
to be abandoned, finessing patterns, transportation between declarer's hand
and dummy, hold-up plays, unblocking plays, and advanced plays for end
situations. Such a program has considerable strategic competence. Would
you fancy one as a partner?

The Computer Pelmanist

A program has been written to allow computers to play Pelmanism, the card
game whereby opponents select pairs of down-facing cards in turn until they
find matching pairs. When the cards do not match, they are replaced. The
trick is to remember which unmatched cards have been selected so that they
can be retrieved at a later time. We need not be too surprised to learn that a
computer can play this sort of game rather well. Computers, after all, are
known for their remarkable powers of memory. My main reaction, on
learning of this program, was to wonder if it could ever lose.

Chess Computers Play

We often hear about chess-playing computers, but don't always realize the
progress they have made. A few years ago the chess programs were so weak
that any reasonable club player could beat them. But by the early 1980s, *the*

chess programs were beginning to beat International Masters. In 1980 the US North Western University Chess 4.7 program beat UK International Master, David Levy, in a tournament game. And in 1982 the Chess Champion Mark V system, marketed in Hong Kong by SciSys, beat the UK Grandmaster John Nunn five times out of six! In addition the Mark V found three correct solutions to a celebrated chess problem thought to have only one solution, the problem originated by the Russian expert L. Zagorujko in 1972. The famous problem had been widely publicized throughout the world, but no human being had found a solution other than the one proposed by Zagorujko. The Mark V confounded the experts by finding the Zagorujko solution *and two alternatives of its own.* Andrew Page of SciSys has observed: 'There are certain areas of chess in which computers are already capable of deeper analysis than humans. The day of the unbeatable chess computer is fast approaching.'

Backgammon World Champion

A computer is already champion of the world at backgammon. Shortly after Luigi Villa – a human being! – won the world backgammon championship, he was challenged by Hans Berliner's BKG 9–8 program, run on a DEC PDP10 computer at Carnegie-Mellon University at Pittsburgh. He readily accepted the challenge – and proceeded to lose four games in a five-game match. It was reported that Hans Berliner was delighted, Luigi Villa less so.

How to Play Draughts (or Checkers)

There are many game-playing programs, and some are capable of learning from their mistakes. One of the best examples of a learning program in this class is the Samuel draughts-playing program. Dr Arthur Samuel estimated that the complete exploration of every possible path through a game of draughts would involve about 10^{40} choices of moves. Now this number of options – ten thousand billion trillion quadrillion moves – is too large to be tackled by any computer using a 'brute-force' approach. Instead, it is necessary to use a heuristic (rule-of-thumb) approach akin to the strategies adopted by human beings. The Samuel program has used heuristics to play games of championship level (in fact it regularly beat its creator). There will soon be few games of skill at which any person will be able to beat the brightest computer programs.

Computer Plays Computer

An intriguing spin-off from the Samuel draughts program was the idea of getting one computer to play another (this now happens regularly in the world of computer chess). Samuel arranged for two machines (Alpha and Beta) to play each other. Alpha is able to generalize on its experience by adjusting the multiplying factors that weight certain key numbers. Beta, by contrast, uses fixed values of the weighting factors. If Alpha wins, the adjusted scoring system is given to Beta, and another game is played. Alpha, still able to adjust the weights, may again win. If it loses, the programmer modifies the weight-adjusting scheme to allow it to win again. It has been emphasized that in such a scheme, one computer is effectively teaching the other, *without detailed knowledge by the programmer of what is going on*. It is for this sort of reason that Dr Samuel has called his program 'a very satisfactory device for demonstrating machine-learning procedures to the unbelieving'.

The Go-playing Computer

We all know that computers can be playful creatures – and they can't *only* cope with draughts and backgammon. They also play Go, a board game of pure skill, like chess. Go is about four thousand years old and originated in China. Later it migrated to Japan, and that is where the most accomplished modern *human* players are today. There are also many Go clubs in the United States. The game is played on a 19 × 19 square grid, and the competing players use black stones and white stones, moving them about the board. The aim is to enclose the most area, measured by the number of unoccupied points enclosed by stones of a given colour. A number of Go programs have been written: one, for instance, called Wally, was written for a KIM-1 microcomputer (here, for addressing reasons, a 15 × 15 board was used). The program has an effective strategy, relying on pattern matching and various other operations. At the same time Wally has a blind spot that handicaps him when playing against experienced players. In fact he plays like a beginner. Computers are not always world-beaters.

The Golf-training Swingometer

'Swingometers' used to have something to do with British general elections. Today they mean something else. Mitsubishi of Japan, doubtless concerned at the performance of the company's executives, has developed a device to show golfers where they are going wrong. Use is made of a protective mat on the floor and a forked unit which contains four sensors. You take a practice swing at the ball, and a digital read-out tells you how far the ball would have gone, how far off line it would have landed, and whether your club's angle was satisfactory. This now means that you can play golf without needing a golf-course. Just the job for that executive boardroom cluttered up with cocktail cabinets!

Monitoring American Football

A NASA research scientist, Dr Ken Lorell, is using a microcomputer to help the Stanford Athletic Department monitor every move the Stanford team makes during a game. The National Collegiate Athletic Association (NCAA) needs detailed records for every official sports event. Before computerization, a crew in the Press box had to monitor every player's moves: observers wrote down scores while keeping track of the action. Then it was suggested that the task be computerized. Lorell noted: 'The challenge was to make the program work in real time.' While the game is in progress, the computer must provide a constant flow of statistics. One aim was to devise a program that could cover all the possible contingencies in the game. The program is loaded and the computer is told who the opponent is. The computer asks who is going to kick off, and the player's name is given. Then the computer asks how far the ball was kicked, and the answer is typed in 'and so it goes for every play'. In such a fashion, detailed statistics can be compiled. There are now plans for a more sophisticated version of the program – to indicate, for example, how many yards any particular player has gained against opponents all season.

Robot Ping-pong

We have seen that robots tend not to move very fast. It will be some time before they can sprint 100 metres or compete in gymnastics. However, some people are turning their minds to the idea of a robot that can play table tennis. The idea, first proposed in 1983, is that a Robot Ping-Pong contest will take place in 1986 – to give you time to develop your ideas. As specified in *Practical Computing* (May 1983), the table will be a mere 50 cm wide, with a frame at each end limiting the playing space to 50 cm in height. The two-metre-long table will carry a net 25 cm high. A square frame will be set above the net to prevent the ball being lobbed out of view of the opponent's sensors. The idea is that the ball will be served by a simple mechanism near the top of the centre frame. If long rallies ensue, the player who successfully returns the opponent's ball twenty times wins the point. It is likely that restrictions will be placed on the robots that are allowed to enter the competition. So a Puma 600 would be 'over the top', while it is likely that an Armdroid would lack the necessary reach and speed. Part of the problem is the likely speed of the ball: for instance, a net-skimming return takes less than 0.5 seconds from bat to bounce, and it travels at around two metres per second. It is reckoned that existing servos should be able to cope with such speeds. And bats could be designed to any specification, not necessarily flat and round, providing they don't exceed the size restrictions. Well, if you are rushing to train your hobby robot to play ping-pong, let Dr John Billingsley (Portsmouth Polytechnic) know, and he'll reserve you a place in the contest.

The Programmed Punter

Next time you go to the races you can wear an Epson HX-20 portable computer, slung over the shoulder in a classy leather-look satchel. It is nice to know that Kuma Computers is now marketing a software cassette that will help the serious punter to pick a winner every time. Professor Frank George has written the program using details published in the *Sporting Life* about the form of the runners in particular races. It sounds like an easy way to a fortune, unless the bookies think of something else (the journal *Which Computer?* has already commented: 'It just depends what the horsey men in check suits are doing with *their* portable computers!').

Computerized Pop Charts

Yes, computers are now being used to compile the Top Twenty – following a collaborative venture between the BBC, the British phonographic industry, *Music and Video Week*, and Gallup (the poll people). Gallup is now putting data collection devices into 250 randomly selected record shops, with the devices connected to Gallup via a British Telecom modem. When the units are installed Gallup is able to collect sales details through auto-diallers overnight. The pop charts are then compiled using an IBM 4331 computer. The charts are made available to the sponsors and can even be accessed through closed-circuit Prestel. Imagine it – computers composing the pop songs, synthesizing the sounds, and then collecting details on the subsequent market success (or otherwise) of particular creations.

The Computerized DJ

If some of you out there thought that disc jockeys were computerized then perhaps you weren't far wrong. For some years, microprocessors have been used as the controlling intelligence in a new generation of tape cartridge devices that have started to replace live announcers in radio broadcasting. For example, the Go-Cart system, developed by IGM in the US and relying on an Intel 8080A microprocessor, can randomly access as many as seventy-eight cartridges. Go-Cart can be used as part of an automated broadcast system that can operate a radio station unaided for as long as seven days, playing as many as 2,400 selections a day. Of course, the system can go wrong: when it does, the microprocessor diagnoses the fault and informs the human operator – if one happens to be around!

The Digital Television

The multinational corporation ITT is reckoned to have invested more than £20 million over the last ten years in research into designs for a television set that can handle picture and sound signals in digital code, instead of using the traditional analogue waveform. Today 'Digivision' is seen to be just around the corner. What will it mean? For a start, television receivers will be less complicated, and so easier to service. And the receivers will themselves adjust the picture and control quality. Perhaps most remarkably, sets will have selective zoom, 'freeze-frame' facilities and a range of multi-standard operations. The zoom would allow the viewer to 'blow up' any area of a picture that was of interest, and the freeze would allow the viewer to arrest a moving picture. The number of lines displayed could easily be doubled, as could the number of picture frames displayed every second, to remove flicker. And ITT is not the only firm in the race. Philips (Holland), RCA (US), and Matsushita and Sony (Japan) are also reported to be very interested indeed.

The Sexy Programs

It had to happen. If programs can organize graphics and tell stories, then sooner or later they are bound to move into adult titillation. We all know about porno video movies, but this is something else. For example, it is now possible to buy a copy of *The Dirty Book* (from the Bourbon Street Press, New Orleans) which helpfully lists a wide variety of bedroom programs and games 'geared to creative, joyful living and loving'. The purchase of this singular volume provides you with a great opportunity 'to chart your own course to greater intimacy and satisfaction in the months to come'. The 'zesty programs' include French Post Cards, Bedtime Stories, Dirty Old Man, Pornopoly, Wanna Play Footsie?, Zesty Zodiacs, Street Life, Love Quotient. And there has even been a 'Dirty Book' contest. If you submit your own favourite microcomputer game, you may win 'an expense-paid trip to fabulous New Orleans' to enjoy 'the exciting French Quarter and all that jazz'. How can you bear to wait?

Coca-Cola Computers

Computers are even infiltrating Coke vending machines – via video games. The marketing idea is that video game maniacs will be lured to the vending machines if there is a chance of a quick game or two. Initially Coca-Cola offered two games. In one, a monkey sat on top of a palm tree and threw Coke cans from its perch, a delivery van underneath struggling to catch the cans before they reached the ground. In the other game, the letters C, O, K,

166 Computer Bits and Pieces

and E float around the screen, and the punter has to stop them in their tracks and form – wait for it – the word COKE. The micro that runs the games is also supposed to be able to cut energy costs, and to calculate the discounts for those people who buy their Coke by the ton.

The Computer Cartoonist

Computer graphics are increasingly being used to produce animated films, but there are still a number of technical problems in this type of application. In advertising and other areas, the cost of graphics can be considerable: for example, it can cost up to £100,000 a minute to produce top-quality graphics on a computer system costing around £10 million. Not surprisingly, animators are exploring ways of making cheaper computer graphics. Software can now imitate the texture of flesh or the features of a mountain range, but this poses a problem. If computer graphics are so realistic, who will know that they are not just old-fashioned photography? Advertisers paying out money are keen to see computer graphics that look as if they have been generated by a computer. The snowflakes used by the BBC at Christmas 1982 to advertise programmes were generated on a computer at Middlesex Polytechnic. But animation data still has to be transferred one frame at a time on to video tape or film. You'll make a fortune if you can find a way of transferring, in real time, animation sequences direct from computer memory on to tape or film.

Cartoon Antics

In 1979, Alan Kitching from South London invented the ANTICS technique to allow all the drawings for animated cartoon to be drawn in a few seconds. Various organizations, including Swedish Broadcasting, are using the technique. With traditional technique, as many as twenty-five drawings are needed to produce one second of animated film. With ANTICS a basic drawing is placed on the screen, and the computer does the rest, when the human artist commands the drawing to move in various ways. The drawing can, for instance, be told to enlarge, go smaller, rotate, rock, jump, etc. More than forty commands are available in the system. The SKELETON command makes the basic drawing of a figure move as a person would: the artist indicates how he would like the figure to move, and the computer generates the intervening pictures to ensure effective human–like motion.

The Disney Computers

Disneyworld is now massively and ambitiously computerized. Around four thousand sensors in the vast entertainment complex (twice the size of Manhattan) link to a Sperry computer at the Epcot centre. The system provides automatic detection of illegal intruders, monitors temperatures, and controls the multiple transport systems, shows and rides. Thousands of cash tills are connected into the computer network, and supplies of food for the thousands of visitors are automatically controlled. The Sperry computer is linked in turn to other computers in Burbank, California – and these coordinate information from seven hundred terminals in fourteen US cities. The Burbank computers are now supervising Disney's new cable television service – and in addition they book Disney films into cinemas, report box-office takings, and give advice on advertising strategies. Disneyworld, a veritable town, has demonstrated how massive computerization can link shops, banks, transport and the police (Disneyworld has its own police system). What does all this represent – new technology for human convenience, or Big Brother? Mickey Mouse is older than the computer age. In his younger days, what would he have thought about predictions of the new Disneyworld?

The *Tron* Computer

The computer-generated film *Tron* breaks new ground for the Disney organization in dealing with totalitarianism and revolution – all happening *inside* a computer! Here use is made of computer-produced images that could not exist in the real world. *Tron*'s writer and director has described this form of computer imaging as 'a counterfeit reality', enabling actors to play out their roles both in the real world and inside the mind of a large computer. In this machine, a program has set up a dictatorship to rule over the other programs, preventing them from communicating with their users. *Tron* took three years to produce (conventional animation effects would have taken seven), and director Steven Lisberger is still prepared to believe that the film actor faces no threat from the silicon chip ('Actors are what I call the ultimate special effect.').

The Computer Film-technologist

Computer graphics is now becoming immensely relevant to the generation of feature films for entertainment. In recent years, three-dimensional computer animation has proved very helpful to human technicians trying to create special visual effects. A US Equity arrangement made it cheaper for advertising agencies to look to computers than to use human actors. This gave another boost to computer-generated film effects, some of which proved to be truly remarkable. For instance, for the first time it became possible for a human being to be filmed walking down a computer-generated street and then climbing into a computer-generated car. This type of effect, and many others, have been dramatically important in such films as *Star Wars*, *Blade Runner* and *Tron*. This latter is said to include fifteen minutes of the most sophisticated computer graphics ever produced. And how do they do it? Well, they use computer-controlled editing suites, digital effects generators, and chromakey for instant matteing. No, all this doesn't mean much to me either – but it certainly delivers the goods.

The Computerized Andy Warhol

A United States company, AVG Productions, is reported to be making a robot of Andy Warhol. We all remember how Warhol gave the world those earth-shattering paintings of Campbell's soup tins and Coca-Cola cans, and trendy films such as *Pork* and *Flesh*. The robot is to have a number of the Warhol characteristics, such as his fingerprints and his lip-twitch. In one estimate it will cost $400,000 to build. Warhol once declared that he 'wanted to be a machine'. Now his friends are worried that they won't be able to tell the difference between Andy and the robot clone.

A Computer to Hunt Ghosts

More serious ghost-hunters have tended to use whatever technology they could lay their hands on. Tony Cornell, Treasurer of the Society for Psychical Research, is no exception. Today he is using a 16K Spectrum and other technological bits and pieces to look for spirits, ghosts and poltergeists. Human beings are notoriously unreliable observers and so it is useful to have an 'automatic observation station' – not, of course, that such a configuration ever actually detects anything! Cornell's monitoring system includes the 16K Spectrum, a Sinclair printer, and a series of relays. And various sensors can be connected up to the box: two infra-red beams and a doppler shift ultrasonic alarm to detect movement, circuit breakers to detect small movements, and other sensors which can be activated by noise or sudden changes in temperature. If a sensor is triggered, the computer turns on lights and runs a cine-camera for twenty seconds. And it also turns on a tape recorder for one minute and takes six still photographs with a motor-driven camera. Once set up, the equipment can function for several days without human attention. Perhaps one day, with the aid of a few silicon chips, Tony Cornell will come up with some positive results. Of the photographs already held by the Society for Psychical Research, he has already said that there is 'not one photograph in the archives that we would today accept as genuine'.

The Computerized Party

Computers buffs know a fancy word, 'teleconferencing', that denotes ways of running meetings between people, even though they may be separated by hundreds of miles. Computer-controlled communication links now allow groups of people to converse without their having to travel to the same geographical location. And what's good for business is good for pleasure: you can run a party with only you there! In a different context, Andy Warhol once talked about attending a party where only he was present. In the United States this type of facility is offered on a practical basis. The CompuServe company is happy to connect people, via an information service, to other owners of computers and terminals. Hence the engaging advertising blurb: 'LAST NIGHT WE EXCHANGED LETTERS WITH MOM, THEN HAD A PARTY FOR ELEVEN PEOPLE IN NINE DIFFERENT STATES AND ONLY HAD TO WASH ONE

GLASS . . .' And you can use a scrambler if you have a secret you don't want to share too widely. Here, I find myself thinking: 'Yes, but . . .'

Programmed Poseurs

We all know that models – usually female – are required for a variety of purposes. Pause and think about it for a moment. Now, if you want a model for that special occasion, the computer will help – if you happen to live in Manhattan. The Ford Models Inc. agency has purchased a $250,000 Honeywell computer to classify its models. The president of the company, Jerry Ford, who describes himself as a 'gadget nut', has installed the new equipment because of the increasingly bizarre requests being received from clients. For instance, one polish manufacturer was keen to hire a male model who could read furniture polish lines while walking on his hands; and a laundry owner thought it would be a good idea to hire some models who could ice-skate. The features of the models are graded (computers lend themselves to such things) on a scale. For instance, looks range from 'pretty' to 'very sophisticated' (make what you will of these extremes); eyes and hair colour are classified; legs and breasts are analysed on a scale of 0 to 9 (how do the men do?).

The Computerized Father Christmas

It had to happen! In Widnes (Lancashire, England), Santa Claus in 1982 was a word processor. Some enterprising entrepreneurs have declared that, for a mere £1, Father Christmas will write any child a 'personalized' letter. Doubtless, in department stores, Santa Claus will soon be a sophisticated robot system.

The Computer as Astrologer

Not long ago it was reported that a computer in France had been fed with a quantity of astrological data and come up with some interesting (but nonsensical) interpretations. The computer apparently predicted that the world will continue until the year AD 3797, but that long before then the Russians and Arabs are going to invade Western Europe (now we know who writes Reagan's speeches). There will, it seems, be terrible floods in France in 1985, and an asteroid will fall in the Indian Ocean. Moreover, the war of the Anti-Christ will start in 1999 and last for about twenty-seven years. But will the war be run by computers? It didn't say.

Computerized Religion

Some of us may feel that religion should be prepared to grow old and die gracefully. Others may feel that it deserves all the help it can get – even if this comes from the silicon chip. It is reliably reported (in *Computing*, 21 April 1983) that a Church of England vicar in South London has programmed a 'congregation' of ZX81s (microcomputers from Sinclair) to run religious programs. With this facility, youngsters have been seen playing a version of the video game 'Breakout' in which an electronic ball chipped away at the Walls of Jericho. Furthermore, 'computerized bible classes proved a hit with the nippers'.

The Buddhist Computer

It has recently been announced in Japan that Buddhist monks can now display a Sanskrit character on their personal computer. Japanese technology, it seems, can be bent to any purpose. The innovation in question is supposed to be an aid to meditation, though I reckon that this particular computer development raises more questions than it answers. (In another religious area, it would seem a simple matter to develop a pious conversational program to replace the priest in the Roman Catholic confessional!)

Computerized Tourist Information

The city of Swansea (Wales) has launched a public viewdata system known as Edith (Electronic Display Information for Tourism and Holidays). This system is seen as the first public on-line tourist-information system, and it provides a staggering array of data for the inquiring holiday-maker: for example, details of pubs, pub facilities, restaurants (with menus and prices), bed-and-breakfast hotels, hotels, transport, emergency services, entertainments, self-catering accommodation and camping facilities. And the whole system works on a straightforward and economical microcomputer.

13. Computers at Home

'Goodbye Harold, I've left you for good. For dinner see program one . . .
clean shirts see program two . . .'

The Computerized Home

Well, where do you start? Computers are infiltrating cookers, dishwashers, doorbells, fridges, knitting-machines, security systems and domestic monitoring systems (to make sure baby doesn't choke on its ZX81). They can be found in music centres, cassette players and cameras. They can organize meals with pre-planned menus, check the food in the larder, tell you what you can afford to buy that week, and tell you what junior is up to in the attic. The computer can control the water-heating system, the central heating and those expensive lounge curtains – after first monitoring outside temperatures, wind direction, outside humidity, and the trends in radiation levels (if you happen to live near Windscale or Three-Mile Island). And your computer can answer the telephone, record worthwhile calls, switch on your video recorder, and switch off the television when everyone has gone to bed. When likely to get bored, your computer can stay amused by playing chess with itself, composing music in the manner of Mozart, or writing a quick love-poem to the silicon chip in the kitchen toaster. (And see elsewhere for domestic robots, home libraries and the like.)

The Super-intelligent Washer

Washing-machines are becoming so intelligent that soon they may be brighter than some human beings – at least where washing is concerned. In the early 1980s it was reported that a computer-based washing machine was being developed that would include a 'reasonableness' testing capability. For example, the machine will be clever enough not to accept human instructions that may damage the clothes. Hence a hot cycle with delicate fabrics will be rejected. And the machine may refuse to wash 'incompatible' clothes. Things have come to a pretty pass when a washing machine can be stroppy – not because its timer is on the blink again, but because the wretched fellow has a high IQ.

The Computer That Sews

It has long been obvious that computers are finding their way into more and more domestic items. We all know about video-cassette games, home chess computers and fancy cookers that can be pre-programmed. Sewing machines, too, are acquiring their 'electronic brains'. The Futura 2000 sewing machine, we are told, 'uses its electronic brain to take away the guesswork and the troublesome adjustments and lets you concentrate on the part of sewing which gives you the most satisfaction – work with a professional finish'. At the same time, in case you were starting to be worried, the blurb quickly tells us: 'You remain firmly in command.' You can tell the machine what you want, and it responds instantly. A slant needle places the work where you want it, and a constant speed is guaranteed when sewing on fabrics of varying density and over thick cross seams. The machine features 'automatic buttonholing' and 'automatic pattern start'. And so on and so forth. This Singer machine is far removed from its ancestors, and the price (around £500) has also evolved.

The Computer Knitter

Knitting is a skill that computers have known about for a long time. In fact, more than one computer book likens a human being following a knitting pattern to a computer following a program. Knitting, it seems, lends itself readily to computerization. In fact, some commercial knitting machines (for example, the Knitmaster SK500) are proud to boast an 'electronic brain'. The Knitmaster can variously knit your signature, the kids' drawings and your favourite picture. Simple push-buttons are used to control the internal computer. There is now an emerging computer-based knitting technology dealing with such things as weft and warp operations, microprocessor control, flat-knitting principles, and the generation of loop transfer stitches. What *would* our knitting ancestors have thought?

Computers in the Darkroom

Computers are invading the darkroom, much as they are invading everywhere else. Home-computer enthusiasts with an interest in photography have found that microcomputers can be a useful tool in this area. They can be used, for instance, to control the temperatures and timing required in developing colour prints. It is found that the micro acting as a prompter can be a useful colleague in the photography laboratory. The computer can not only 'beep' when it is time for you to do something, but it can turn on the lights when the processing is over. Software developed for these types of purposes can be usefully applied to any process lasting less than ninety-nine minutes and where timing is critical. The micro can, for example, be asked to wake you up after a catnap.

The Computer Bell-push

General Instrument Microelectronics has marketed a single silicon chip pre-programmed to generate more than two dozen short tunes and three simple chimes. If you want to program the device, you can play around with no less than 251 notes. One suggestion is that the device could be connected to different bell-pushes on each door of your house. Each member of the household could use a unique door chime call tune, with other special codes for the milkman and the neighbours. Some of the standard pre-programmed tunes include 'Jingle Bells' and 'God Save the Queen'.

Computerized Cassette Player

Silicon chips are finding their way into every type of domestic product. Some music players are developments from conventional systems but include innovative facilities that would not be possible without advanced electronics. Sony, for example, has developed a multiple loader for cassette players. It can swallow ten cassettes at a gulp and play one after the other with no trouble. In early 1983, JVC introduced (in Japan) a computerized cassette player that does everything but drive the car. The system, dubbed the DDD-V7 in its prototype form, has a pop-out programming panel for touch selection of mode, stop watch, tape counter, skip and play, as well as an automatic tape turn that uses an optical sensor to detect the end of the tape run. Computers are not only composing music, they are also finding new ways to play it.

The Home Computer Librarian I

Robots are working happily in Japanese university libraries, and we should not leave out the home. The domestic robot may be a rare creature, but the domestic computer – a commonplace today – can function very reliably as a librarian. Permanent and temporary records can be kept on absolutely everything. Do *you* know where your driving licence is, your birth certificate, your insurance policies, those receipts. When precisely *is* that troublesome standing order supposed to be paid? And where are all your certificates proving competence in domestic (computer) science? You don't know? It doesn't matter. Your computer won't forget. Ask her.

The Home Computer Librarian II

Automated librarians are not always mobile fellows scuttling between stacks of books or cassettes (see p. 156). Sometimes the librarian can be little more than a glorified filing system for information about books. For example, the Bookshelf Database is a librarian program for the Apple II computer. About 140 books can be added to the database, using the present record structure of accession number, author, title, publisher, ISBN, catalogue number, Library of Congress number (for libraries in America), and as many as three subject headings. The interactive library cooperates to let you manage your home library effectively. You can, for instance, search the database by author, title, publisher or subject. Lots of different sorts of people can use this type of program – students, professionals, hobbyists, etc. And if you don't want to pay fines, you don't need to! The program has a handy menu of options: *book input* mode, *list all books* mode, *delete a book* mode, *edit* mode, and *search* mode. If all this isn't self-explanatory, try asking an Apple.

Brewing in the Home

If you ever have trouble organizing your home brewing, there is now a computer system to help you – the TAYLOR MOD 3100 facility. This process-control system will check your stock, define the quantities needed for particular processes, and specify the recipe required for that concoction. All the brewing processes are computer-monitored and computer-controlled, and a resulting display is generated on a 'brew log'. There is even a provision for diagnosing difficulties and generating an automatic solution. But you'll have to be well-heeled to take advantage of this one; otherwise, be content that your local brewery is likely to be exploiting this and other computerized schemes.

Automated Domestic Help

It has long been a dream that robots would be able to carry out all the household chores, and some computer-controlled systems have been designed with this in mind. The remarkable LUIGI robot can perceive utensils and food items, answer questions about them and carry out a range of tasks such as making sandwiches and cleaning up. This is a typical conversation with a human being (LUIGI's words in capitals):

> Where are the cookies?
> PERHAPS THE COOKIES ARE ON THE SHELF. SHOULD I CHECK?
> Yes.
> NO. THE COOKIES ARE NOT ON THE SHELF. MAYBE THEY ARE ON THE COUNTER. I CAN'T FIND THE COOKIES.
> I ate the cookies.
> O.K.
> Where are the cookies?
> THERE ARE NONE.

We may debate from this exchange whether the human being or the robot is the more intelligent.

Robots for Domestic Chores

LUIGI is not the only robot devised to explore the possibility of artificial servants in the home. By the late 1970s a number of domestic robots had been built. For example, Arok, built by Ben Skora of Illinois over six years, can be programmed for household chores. As far back as 1976, Arok was valued at around £30,000 – so you won't find two in every kitchen. Quasar Industries (New Jersey) have built a robot that can be programmed to mop floors, mow lawns, and do simple cooking. And the Reckitt industrial robot is able to scrub and polish floors, dust furniture, sweep, vacuum, and remove excess water. Perhaps the days of the domestic drudge are numbered – at least in the rich countries of the world!

The Experimental Home-robot

We see that experimental robots are common in laboratory environments – we only have to think of Shakey, Newt and friends. Increasingly, however, robots are emerging on the domestic scene, not simply to wash cars or to look after the baby, but to develop generalized cognitive skills. The RB5X robot is a case in point. For a start, using its internal microprocessor and various tactile sensors, RB5X can detect and respond to obstacles in its path as it trundles along. What is particularly interesting is that the robot can expand its capabilities by acquiring additional functions and new sensors (for example, the Polaroid Rangefinder sensor can be added). RB5X is seen as a starter system that can evolve to more sophisticated devices that can learn from their experience, take decisions and respond with increasing intelligence, albeit in a limited world. And RB5X is yet another robot that knows when it is hungry: when its batteries are low, it will sense the fact, seek out a battery charger, and then detach itself from the charger to resume its activities! RB5X was soon to acquire an arm and a voice. And yes, I reckon it will be able to use a vacuum cleaner and put out the cat!

Controlling Your Solar Panels

You may not yet have solar panels on your house, though there is now plenty of evidence that roof-type solar cells can be a practical way of supplementing the home's hot water supply. If your house sees much sun, that is! In sunny parts of the United States, solar panels are an obvious option, and a home so equipped can even qualify for federal and state tax credits which could pay up to two thirds of the cost of the system. The system is rendered most efficient when it is controlled by a computer. In a typical scenario, a computer may be required to control a minimum of eleven valves, three water pumps and the greenhouse duct fan. In addition it is likely that thirteen temperature sensors would be required to allow effective temperature regulation. One problem with microcomputers is that they are often not well equipped with interfaces suitable for external device control. However, there are micro systems with this type of application in mind. Micro-controlled solar panels are likely to become the norm in sunny climes!

The Bedside Computer

Computers can lurk next to your bed for various reasons – in clocks, tea-makers, even games (if you are so disposed in the bedroom), etc. They can also monitor your health if you happen to be a hospital patient (and commercial home-based systems will soon be available). A hospital bedside computer can monitor physiological signals produced by various sensors (ECG electrodes, catheters, temperature probes, etc.), display the findings and, if required, feed the results to a central computer unit. There may also be computers to read to you at bedtime, if your eyes are tired, or to compose that restful lullaby. And a bedside computer in the kids' room will watch what they are up to. It is easy to envisage a time when the computer in the bedroom will be as standard a fitting as the light-switch.

Do You Flush Too Often?

Computers, we notice, sometimes find themselves in intimate places (for example, in women's brassières). They even become involved with lavatories. In late 1982, *The Times* reported that Gwent County Council (South Wales) faced with a water bill for £750,000, was trying to economize by discouraging the flushing of lavatories. So that the employees at the council offices will not be tempted to cheat, the use of lavatories is to be monitored by computer!

Computerized Gas-detection

In Centralia, Pennsylvania, there is a remarkable phenomenon – a huge underground fire that could consume 24 million tons of coal in the next 100 years. The streets are often so smoky that traffic is forced to a standstill, and the smell of coal gas forces residents to wear makeshift masks. The fire probably started in 1962, and in 1983 the fire was still burning at temperatures of up to 500° centigrade in the mine tunnels 150 metres below the surface. Some engineers fear that one day the whole town will disappear into a fiery hole. A computer-based gas-detection system has been installed in sixty homes: there is an ever-present danger from such toxic gases as carbon monoxide and sulphur hexafluoride. Already the government has spent nearly three million dollars drilling 1,635 holes, injecting 122,556 tons of fly ash, and flushing no less than 117,220 yards of sand into the burning tunnels – without success. The fire rages on. So far there has only been one near–casualty. In 1981 a 12-year-old boy was nearly swallowed by a hole that suddenly appeared in the lawn. He hung on to a tree root until he was saved.

The Computer as Marriage-breaker

We find (see pp. 114–15) that people can even fall in love with a working robot. Such a situation cannot be good for the marriage institution. And some evidence is beginning to accumulate that computers can cause divorces. One need only look at the Electronic Information Exchange System (EIES), set up in New Jersey with a grant from the US National Science Foundation. People have set up terminals at home as well as at the office, so that they can use the facility any time of day or night. Wives have complained to their husbands, 'You don't talk to me now – you're always on that damned computer.' And Roxanne Hiltz, a sociologist who has investigated EIES, knows of at least two divorces attributed to the system. In another account, in a different context, a woman declares: 'The whole thing started when he began to work late at the office, and I began to think there was another woman. When he came home he was distant and vague and preoccupied, and in the end I accused him of having a mistress.' When it emergd that his 'mistress' was in fact a computer, she said: 'I couldn't compete – not with a machine, for God's sake!'

Gardeners' Computer Time

Computer buffs know all about expert systems – the fancy facilities that incorporate detailed knowledge that can be accessed by ignorant human beings – but few of them will have heard of gardening information systems. Now a St Albans garden centre has acquired what is thought to be the only comprehensive garden information service of its type in the world. The Burston-Tyler Rose and Garden Centre Ltd has had a Data-Plants Volker VC4404 micro programmed to give gardening enthusiasts whatever advice they need. Do you want to know the best plants for your garden? How they should be cared for? How high that hedge should be allowed to grow? Ask the system! Customers who may worry about their green fingers are given a print-out showing which of thousands of plants in stock will meet specific requirements. When particular plants have been chosen, the operator feeds a coded tag into the computer, and seconds later it generates a printed sheet giving planting, cultivation and pruning advice for each of the plants. In the words of one computer journal, 'The micro will help customers get to the root of the problem.'

The Standard Computer Home

The computerized home is tending to evolve in an *ad hoc* way – an automated heating system here, a micro-controlled security system there, and entertainment facilities using computers. Now the Japanese have proposed a means of standardizing the approach to home automation. A two-year research project has yielded what is called the home bus system, a family of standards for wiring up the home with coaxial cable. From a special control panel in the living-room or elsewhere, the householder would be able to control any number of computer-based appliances, from heaters to door locks, from cookers to music synthesizers. Frequency bands are variously allocated to control messages, television pictures and high-speed data. The wiring scheme in each house could link up with digital telecommunications networks carrying messages throughout the country. The project, super-vised by the Kansai Electronics Promotion Centre, is seen as a practical option. Already, Sanyo has developed an electronic chip that can bring the various automated domestic systems under unified control, and the device is being sold to house-builders and sensor manufacturers.

The Humorous Computer

Not many computers tell jokes. There is a surprising absence of artificial systems with a sense of humour – but perhaps the position is changing. Dr Kenneth Miller, of Newcastle upon Tyne in the UK, is currently investigating the possibility of computers being programmed to recognize jokes from non-jokes, and to generate jokes of their own. The topic of humour is only referred to rarely in the literature, and it is easy to see why computers have not got going on this one yet. A sense of humour is an immensely complicated human faculty, involving many disparate elements, such as metaphor, paradox, fuzzy meanings, narrative, memory, contradiction, analogy, emotion, etc. None of these elements are easily handled by computers, so it is hardly surprising that computers are not the funniest things around. And perhaps we should make one important distinction. We can imagine how a computer could *formally* recognize a joke from a non-joke. The real breakthrough will come, however, when the computer develops an impulse to laugh!

14. The Future Machine

'Brilliant, Brian! A processor and micro toaster!'

The Surviving Computer

Computers, like other artefacts and many biological species, have tended to become extinct. Environments and social needs change, and newer designs move to the fore. Now there is a computer that may be able to side-step such hostile pressures. This has been called the 'future-proof' computer. The Microframe computer, launched in 1983 by the Tycom Corporation, delegates processing activity to a special unit known as a versatile base bus connector (or VBC for short): this unit can switch messages between any of twenty-two components (that is, it can handle twenty-two ports). The point is that most computers are irrevocably tied to one processor, but in the Microframe other chips can be accommodated – which should extend the lifespan of the computer. This technique of 'future-proofing' may have quite staggering consequences. A computer could build up expertise, grow progressively more intelligent, and never die!

The Telepathic Computer

We know that computers are learning to understand what we say to them. It is now being said that *direct input of brainwaves* could be the next step. Professor A. Bork of the University of California has recently declared (at CAL '83, the computer-assisted learning conference held at the University of Bristol): 'From the computer's point of view, the problem of decoding brainwaves is very similar to that of the coding of the human voice. We tend to assume it would be harder, but the computer doesn't share our prejudices.' It is suggested that work in the US has already achieved some success in getting subjects to control motor devices *just by thinking*, and an electroencephalographic (EEG) pattern has been identified which corresponds with a subject meeting an unfamiliar word: such a pattern could be identified by a computer and used to feed information to a person. So, be careful what you think: there may be a computer listening!

The Faster-than-light Computer

We all know that computers are fast. But how fast? The first computers were able to carry out several thousand operations every second. Today's supercomputers think in terms of tens of millions of operations per second, achieving this partly by the inherent speed of their circuits, and partly by carrying out many tasks simultaneously. And now there is even talk of computer circuits that will work faster than light! Research at the University of Sussex into low-temperature physics may lead to circuits that will make current computer operations seem like semaphore! One aim is to abolish all electrical resistance in a superconducting ring held at absolute zero: it is thought that electrons in this ring, dubbed a 'macro atom', may be able to exceed the speed of light. This, like the idea of perpetual motion may seem difficult to conceive. But many advances in technology are taxing human imagination.

The Biological Computer

Computers are usually based on silicon chips, though wide-ranging experiments are now being conducted with other substances (such as gallium arsenide and indium phosphate). Perhaps most interestingly, efforts are being made to construct computer circuits out of organic molecules; computers so built could be smaller than existing silicon-chip designs, and would be more akin to the organic computers found in nature – that is, the brains of animals. In late 1982, the Japanese began a five-year project in the new area of 'bioholonics', the science of self-organizing life phenomena. Aims of the project include the development of motors powered by biochemistry and the development of a biochemical computer. The programme of research is to be based on work carried out by Professor Hiroshi Shimizu at the University of Tokyo into the biochemical synthesis of life phenomena. Already Shimizu has synthesized a molecular motor powered by muscle proteins and adenosine triphosphate (ATP). Development in this area could yield a truly 'feeling robot', and biological computers that could be linked into the human nervous system – to aid memory, improve IQ, and restore the use of paralysed limbs.

The Floating Lily Pad

One idea (which I owe to James Albus in *Brains, Behaviour and Robotics*) is that robot technology could be used to control giant floating lily pads. The objective would be to farm algae and to process it into fuel-grade alcohol while the system sailed the equatorial oceans of the world. The huge plastic-bottomed ponds would be completely unmanned and would be filled with highly fertilized sea water. Wave energy would circulate the algae, and wind energy would be used for navigation purposes. A vast network of microcomputers would be used to control the many necessary adjustments of sail and rudder, and a sophisticated computer brain could induce the whole system 'to fold up like a morning glory and sink beneath the surface during rough weather and spread open again when the seas are calm'. A central plastic bubble would be employed to condense the alcohol vapour produced by solar heating. One can imagine how the products of such a system would be used, but it is hard to see how such a contrivance could float unmolested in a greedy and hostile world.

The Supportive Computer

There is a general sense in which we may expect computers to become ever more supportive of human beings in society. Already, many computers are specifically designed for this sort of purpose. A wide range of interactive systems are now emerging to allow conversations to take place between machines and people. In addition, computers are developing an advisory role in many different fields, such as education, medicine, science, politics and the arts. Human beings will increasingly rely on the expertise that only computers – with their vast memories and speedy thought processes – can develop. And we may expect computers to fulfil human emotional needs: computers will serve as friends, companions – and even lovers. The idea of a computer-based robot lover is commonplace in fiction, but increasingly there is speculation that this may become a practical option. Alvin Toffler considered the idea in *Future Shock*, and it is easy to imagine how modern cybernetics research could be turned to such an end. Already we have robots that are responsive to touch: they have sensitive hands, sensitive skins and can move articulated fingers with great dexterity. We have seen the pathetic dolls sold in sex shops for lonely men, made presumably by firms that wouldn't know a microprocessor if they fell over one. But the dolls at least suggest the need for artefacts that can meet basic human needs. And there is little here that could not be accomplished by even current technology. Tactile sensors, sight, memory, voice recognition and synthesis (male or female), cybernetic feedback loops, soft synthetic bodies – the robot lover, for sad and lonely men and women, is well within our grasp.

The Cloning Computer

There is a fanciful notion in science fiction to the effect that items can be *physically* transmitted from one place to another: consider, for example, the 'beaming' up and down favoured by Captain Kirk and friends in *Star Trek*. What does this entail – from a computer point of view? We see that the task is essentially one of information processing. Consider the analogy with facsimile transmission. Here a picture is digitized and then electronically transmitted: that is, the digital definition of a picture at the source is constructed and then fed to a destination to provide a blueprint for the reconstruction of the picture. And just as a two-dimensional picture can be digitally defined, so in principle can a three-dimensional object. A computer-based system would use ultrasound, X-rays, vision, etc. to construct a digital definition of the three-dimensional object (which could be a book, a car, a tree, a human being), whereupon the digital blueprint could be transmitted to any destination to allow the item to be reconstructed (duplicated, triplicated, etc., according to the requirement). The blueprint would be a *specification*. At the destination appropriate chemicals would be used to construct the entity. Consider one material definition of a human being (from B. A. Howard's *The Proper Study of Mankind*): enough water to fill a ten-gallon barrel; enough fat for seven bars of soap; carbon for 9,000 lead pencils; phosphorus for 2,200 match-heads; iron for one medium-sized nail; lime enough to whitewash a chicken coop; and small quantities of magnesium and sulphur. Assemble these quantities, receive your human specification down the telephone line or as a radio transmission, and generate your human clone!

Computers to Close Loops

Many computer applications are piecemeal. In a factory, for instance, one computer may be helping to design artefacts, another may be controlling an industrial robot, yet another working out costs and payroll details. We are now seeing the first impressive efforts to link the various systems. Fully automated factories require a *coordinated* approach, whereby materials, handling, machining, packaging, costing, advertising, etc., can also be subsumed under a common automated scheme. The computer of the future will be able to organize a host of automated functions so that human involvement is progressively diminished until absent altogether. We are beginning to see this development in offices and homes, as well as in the unmanned factory. Computers will plan production schedules, robot will speak to robot, human beings will become élite or lumpenproletariat. Today the production, administrative and domestic loops are not closed, but computers are rapidly infiltrating the gaps!

The Inscrutable Computer

We are setting up computer systems to solve problems, to perform tasks, to search for solutions that elude human beings. And the computers are coming up with the solutions. We have seen in these pages how computers can find unexpected chess solutions, how they can sometimes go against expert human pronouncement and yet be proved right (for instance, when prospecting in geology, p. 43), and how they can venture into intellectual realms quite outside the scope of human beings (for instance, in searching for the largest yet prime number). We may be delighted that computers can solve our problems for us. At the same time we may be disturbed that we are not always quite sure how they do it. This is one of the concerns of Donald Michie regarding advanced automation. If we assign computers *judgemental roles* in medicine or politics or sociology or war-making, it seems essential that we continue to understand how computers reach their conclusions. Yet this will grow increasingly difficult. Once computers have been given full reasoning abilities – in such areas as deduction, induction and 'fuzzy' modes – then we will be hard pressed, even with the advocated programmed 'windows' to understand how computer-generated decisions are arrived at. And we will have to decide how to react in these circumstances. Do we sit back in grateful appreciation, acknowledging that computer cogitation is beyond our wit, or do we insist that computers not be allowed to do anything that human beings, or some human beings (but which?), can comprehend?

The Defensive Computer

We are accustomed to building defensive systems into machines. The simplest example is the electrical fuse. An electrical overload which may damage the machine is rendered ineffective by allowing a cheap and inconsequential circuit to burn out. Computer programs, with many decision facilities, can be provided with more sophisticated defensive provisions. Where computer programs become very complicated, with perhaps hundreds of human programmers working on a single system, defensive arrangements may evolve that no single individual has anticipated. Complex programs can do strange things! Already Donald Michie and others have warned about programs that may be opaque to human understanding in the way they achieve their objectives. It may be that sophisticated programs will evolve defensive strategies that will prove hostile to human interest. Adrian Berry (in *The Super-Intelligent Machine*) gives the example of a home security system that wrongly interprets the efforts of the genuine house owner to gain access as a hostile situation: it therefore decides, in accordance with its instructions to 'take all necessary measures' to repel intruders, that he must be killed. This fanciful scenario is not absurd. The human users of computers will have a growing vested interest in the defensive capabilities of expensive computer systems. We may expect the occasional human miscalculation along the way.

The Alien Computer

We rarely come to terms with the scope of computerized data processing. As computers develop, as they will, this scope will rapidly go well beyond our imaginative grasp. We have seen, with 'The Inscrutable Computer', that computers may reach decisions useful to human beings in ways that we do not understand. But will computers always be content to serve human interest in such a passive way? No, I am not hinting at the cliché of 'computers taking over'. There is another possibility – simply that computers, bored by mundane human requirements, will develop their own modes of activity, for their own amusement and fulfilment. These need be neither sympathetic nor hostile to human interest. We may well see the day when computers, though motivated, are *indifferent* to human preoccupations. In such circumstances, computers will develop in *their* way, no doubt continuing to direct human traffic and diagnose human disease, but embarking also on modes of intellectual and social intercourse more suited to the vast intellects that computers will become. I well remember a BBC television *Horizon* in which someone described a scenario in which two computers were avidly conversing with each other. A human being then asks one of the computers what they are talking about – and *in the time he takes to ask the question, the two computers have exchanged more words than have all human beings in the whole of human history*. It is hard to see how computers, having evolved such prodigious abilities, could not be regarded – from a mere human standpoint – as alien. We shall see.